God calls his peopl
to choose wise over
Why? Because transformation begins with "the renewing of our minds." What you do with your gray matter matters, and *The Disciple's Mind* shows you: the most faithful believers think wisely and well. More importantly, it shows you *how* to do that—how to "think *about* Jesus, think *like* Jesus, and think *through* Jesus" about all of life. I've known Daniel McCoy and Chad Ragsdale for twenty years, and I can say three things: they're faithful Christ-followers, they're fun and engaging communicators, and you'll find no better guides on "the road less stupid."

—**Matt Proctor**, president, Ozark Christian College

This book is desperately needed. Its incisive analysis of Scripture and society helps to diagnose and destroy a disease that deteriorates our churches and dwarfs our discipleship. Its content is eminently biblical and immensely practical. Its style is creative, entrancing, and even entertaining. Many books are good. This one could make a huge down-to-earth kingdom difference if widely read and intentionally applied.

—**Richard A. Knopp**, PhD, executive director, Room For Doubt; professor emeritus of Philosophy and Christian Apologetics, Lincoln Christian University and Seminary

Many Christians place a great amount of emphasis on biblical morality: what we ought to do and how we should do it. Still, this concern requires that we think about our lives as Christians, which in turn leads us to think about our faith as a whole. On this level there is a great need to keep sound thinking from lapsing into emotionalism or an unreflective dogmatism. Ragsdale and McCoy encourage Christians to avoid traps caused by bad habits of thinking and present us with solid, livable ways of using our minds along scriptural principles. The book flows easily while conveying a profound message. Of particular help are the interesting accounts at the beginning of each chapter, some of which are engagingly written in the venerable genre of allegory.

—**Winfried Corduan**, PhD, professor emeritus of Taylor University, author of *Neighboring Faiths* and *In the Beginning God*

In our day and age, which is dominated by social media, there are innumerable voices vying for our devoted attention. As a result, many people, including Christians, will find themselves drifting in a vast ocean not knowing what truth is or how to discover it. *The Disciple's Mind* is a necessary tool that has come to the rescue. It will help Jesus followers, intellectually, by reinforcing the truth and how to know the truth. But it will also equip disciples to have the heart of Jesus so that others will know the truth, be set free, and have life everlasting.

—**Brian Cunningham**, PhD, pastor and apologist

After spending more than thirty years cultivating faith in young people, I find myself increasingly concerned about the challenges they encounter in today's complex cultural, digital, and political landscapes. Despite the abundance of information and resources at their fingertips, discerning truth in this age is more challenging than ever. The seeming convenience of our era is deceptive; it often masks the underlying complexities, leaving us in a state of confusion and uncertainty. In this context, *The Disciple's Mind* emerges as a crucial guide, blending profound insights with practical, faith-based wisdom.

The modern mind is relentlessly bombarded by competing voices and ideologies, especially online. It's crucial to have a solid foundation to discern truth from deception. This book provides just that foundation, encouraging a deep and thoughtful engagement with God's Word. Ragsdale and McCoy empower us, and especially youth, to critically evaluate the content consumed daily—be it social media, news, or entertainment—and to respond with a faith that is both informed and resilient.

Ragsdale and McCoy integrate faith with intellectual rigor to help us grapple with issues like identity, morality, and purpose. This book equips us to form a biblically sound worldview. It teaches us to appreciate nuance and complexity, to be open-minded yet discerning, and to approach discussions with humility and a desire for understanding. This balanced approach is essential in a cultural landscape polarized by extreme viewpoints and the societal pressure to conform.

In addition, the emphasis on community resonates deeply in a time where isolation and individualism are rampant. The authors place high values on reflection and discussion in the context of conversation. This book highlights the importance of being part of a faith community, where beliefs are not just personal but shared, discussed, and lived out in love and service. This is a powerful antidote to the loneliness and fragmentation that many people experience in their online interactions.

This book is a much-needed anchor in times of shifting values and moral relativism. It encourages engagement with current events and political issues thoughtfully, examining them through the lens of Scripture, and responding with Christ-like compassion and conviction.

As someone who has worked with young people for over thirty years, I can attest to the urgent need for a resource like *The Disciple's Mind*. It's a guidebook for believers to navigate the complexities of their era without compromising their faith. It's a call to love God not just with our hearts and souls, but with our minds—fully, deeply, and actively.

For anyone invested in the spiritual growth and intellectual development of the next generation, *The Disciple's Mind* is an important tool. It is a book that doesn't just inform; it transforms, making it a must-read for anyone dedicated to the discipleship of young Christians in today's challenging world.

—**Jayson French**, president of Christ in Youth

THE DISCIPLE'S MIND

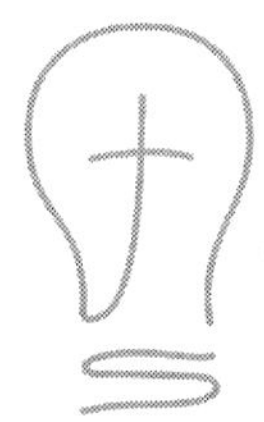

Thinking Like a Disciple of Jesus

CHAD RAGSDALE & DANIEL MCCOY

Requests for information should be sent via email to Renew.org. Visit Renew.org for contact information.

Emphases by the author are in italics.

ISBN: 978-1-959467-27-4 (Paperback)
ISBN: 978-1-959467-28-1 (ePub)

Cover and interior design: Bryana Anderle (YouPublish.com)
Editorial and art direction: Chad Harrington (YouPublish.com)

Contents

Introduction

Ever watched a movie in which A-list actors had to work with a lousy script? You may have left the theater reflecting on how all that money and talent could have blossomed into a blockbuster if the writing had been better.

Ever watch someone do something brainless and ask, "What were you thinking?" only to realize that they *weren't* thinking? Ever find yourself reflecting on something stupid you did, wishing you had started thinking *before* you made the decision?

Taking action without thinking is a bit like playing a movie part without a well-crafted script. Your thinking is the underlying script by which you act your role. If you don't want to be stuck with a lousy script, you need to be more intentional about your thinking.

You have been given a mind. Just as your body, your house, your friendships, and your finances can fall into disrepair through neglect, if you overlook your mind, then your script will go flat. Mindlessness, whether it's based on passionate impulses or robotic routines, can become a rogue GPS that guides you away from your intended route—even off cliffs.

This book is an exploration of the wonderful gift God has given you—your mind—through the lens of following Jesus.

How can we, as disciples of Jesus, use our minds well? How can we avoid mind traps that prevent us from growing and flourishing, often for decades? In the chapters ahead, we'll walk through what it means to love God *with* our minds and what it looks like to let the Holy Spirit guide our thinking. We'll examine how we can think well *and* live morally so that our virtue and intellect don't compete. We'll also discuss how we should think about the culture we live in and how we should think about other Christians.

We've crafted each chapter with a specific framework to guide you through the book:

Imagination and Explanation. Each chapter begins with an imaginative story to help introduce a concept, followed by the more explanation-centered core of the chapter. Exploring each topic from more than one angle will help truths permeate more deeply into your thinking.

Warnings and Invitations. Throughout the book, you will find a combination of warnings to help you guard your mind and invitations to help your mind flourish. There is much to celebrate and explore when it comes to this gift God has given us, even as we stay wary of possible snares.

Reflection and Discussion. Each chapter ends with a section for reflection and discussion containing a thought exercise called "Think It Through" and four questions. There's plenty in each chapter to reflect on, but much of the transformative heavy lifting will be done through the accountability that comes with relationships. That's why we strongly encourage you to walk through this book with other Christians. The core mission of the church is to make disciples of Jesus, and our hope is that this book will be a resource to help you be discipled and disciple others to become more like him.

As Paul explained in 1 Corinthians 2:16, "We have the mind of Christ." It is with the knowledge of this reality and goal that we set out on the following tour of the disciple's mind.

The Dawn and Destination of the Christian Mind

It was time to make the Y-shaped incision, beginning with each shoulder, and then open the body up. Sometimes in autopsies, one quickly sees the unmistakable clues—gunshots, stab wounds, etc.—that explain how the death occurred. But often, an external look is inconclusive, and you have to look deeper.

An autopsy on a dead church almost always requires a deeper, inside look.

I was performing one such church autopsy when I became puzzled. Usually, it wasn't this difficult to find the cause of death.[1] It's not uncommon for a church to succumb to heart disease, having "forsaken the love [they] had at first" (Revelation 2:4). Or maybe it's lung disease, when a church has inhaled carcinogenic beliefs for decades. Sometimes a church body develops auto-immune disorders, and the body attacks its own members as if they are the enemy. There also can be malnutrition, where the body has lived off a steady diet of inspirational experiences that are high in additives and sweeteners and deficient in essential vitamins. However, the corpse in front of me showed none of the usual causes of death.

I examined whether any areas of the body showed signs of age-related failure. Sometimes organs can malfunction or stop working altogether because of age, leaving a crucial function undone. Each organ, however, showed no signs of overuse or chronic stress: heart, kidneys, lungs, and brain. Actually, the brain showed the fewest signs of wear of any organ I checked. No signs of overuse there at all, or even *use* in the first place. It must have been years since it had been activated.

I checked the information chart given to me when the body was brought in. Reading the medical history in light of the brain's inactivity brought a fresh picture into focus. There had been no real scriptural engagement beyond some cherry-picked motivational quotes. There was no cultural awareness, no worldview discernment, and no gospel contextualization. There had been no attempt at apologetics or even theology. A lot of activity, yes, but not the mental kind.

From this autopsy, I learned that, at least with churches, brain death can occur *before*—even years before—a body ceases activity.

* * *

A teacher of the law once tried to test Jesus by asking him to identify the greatest commandment. With brilliant simplicity, Jesus responded with words that would have been familiar to his interrogator because they were borrowed from the Hebrew Scriptures:

> Jesus replied: "'Love the Lord your God with all your heart and with all your soul and with all your mind.' This is the first and greatest commandment. And the second is like it: 'Love your neighbor as yourself.' All the Law and the Prophets hang on these two commandments." (Matthew 22:34–40; see also Mark 12:28–31)

The most important thing for any person, past or present, is the proper ordering of our loves. First, we love God wholly and completely, and then we love our neighbors. Love, in this context, means much more than the vague and fickle feeling of affection that we sometimes call love. The kind of love mentioned in this passage is a total reorientation of our desires, our commitments, and our actions. It gives us a particular way of *seeing* the world and our place in it, forming a distinct worldview.

What does it mean to love God in all three areas—heart, soul, and mind? We should be careful about reading too much into the distinction between heart, soul, and mind in this passage. These verses employ a merism, a figure of speech where the combination of parts is used to refer to the whole. For instance, when we describe a deception with the words "he swallowed it hook, line, and sinker," we mean that someone believed the deception completely. So a person who loves God heart, soul, and mind is a person who loves God completely. With that said, it is still helpful to wonder what it looks like for us to love God with every part of our being. How does a person love God with their heart? How do they love God with their soul or their strength? These are good questions for any disciple to ask.

Let's look at the importance of examining how a person can love God with their whole mind.

Neglecting the Mind

There are three mistakes commonly made by disciples when it comes to the mind. The first mistake is *neglecting the mind.* In Mark Noll's influential book *The Scandal of the Evangelical Mind,* the first line bluntly states, "The scandal of the evangelical mind is that there is not much of an evangelical mind."[2] You might think Noll's assessment is too broad, but among many evangelicals there is a certain resistance to the life of the mind. We'd rather concern ourselves with spirituality or the practical concerns of Christian life and ministry. "Intellectual stuff" is fine for some people, but for the rest of us, it just gets in the way. It's a distraction. The result is that our spirituality becomes disconnected from careful thought, and our practical concerns begin to look suspiciously similar to worldly concerns.

> GOD CREATED US AS RATIONAL BEINGS WHO THINK, REASON, AND BELIEVE.

God created us as rational beings who think, reason, and believe. Thinking isn't incidental to who we are; it is fundamental. Christian philosopher J. P. Moreland says, "The mind is the soul's primary vehicle for making contact with God, and it plays a fundamental role in the process of human maturation and change, including spiritual transformation."[3] This quote echoes Paul's assertation in Romans 12:2 that we are transformed by the renewing of our minds. The call to discipleship also calls us to carefully attend to our minds—how we think, what we think, and why we think. This doesn't mean that every Christian must be a scholar, not at all. But every Christian *does* have a mind that thinks; therefore, every Christian has an obligation to love God with that mind. Neglecting the mind will undoubtedly lead to malformed disciples.

Disconnecting the Mind

The second mistake is related to the first. It is the mistake of *separating the mind from the rest of our discipleship.* It's not that we don't care about thinking. We may care deeply about pursuing knowledge and thinking well. However, some of us have disconnected that pursuit from our lives as disciples. Knowledge is important to us; it just isn't important to our faith. Perhaps we have been seduced by the false dichotomy that sees faith and reason as having little to do with each other.

This dichotomy is proven false because biblical faith is most certainly not irrational or without reason. A verse like 1 Peter 3:15 makes this clear. This verse assumes the reasonableness of our faith in urging us to be prepared to give the reason (*apologia*) for the hope that we have. This dichotomy also misses the crucial fact that our beliefs aren't isolated to our minds; our beliefs give direction to our lives. Moreland puts it well when he calls beliefs "the rails upon which our lives run."[4] What we believe is ultimately seen in our behavior, so loving God with our minds is not just about thinking well. It is about acting well.

Idolizing the Mind

The third mistake is the opposite of the first one, the mistake of *caring about nothing other than the mind.* To put it another way, some of us are at risk of loving our minds rather than loving God *with* our minds.

There is great value in delighting in complicated theological ideas, in diving into the depths of biblical exegesis, historical theology, or philosophical reasoning. Yet there is great danger in detaching the intellect from a heartfelt relationship with God.

Throughout its history, the church has been blessed by rare intellectuals who have gone to unusual lengths to passionately seek after the truth. One of those people was Thomas Aquinas, a careful and thorough thinker who continues to positively influence Christian belief hundreds of years after he lived. Yet Aquinas was also a man of deep personal conviction who prayed this simple prayer each day of his life:

> Grant me, O Lord my God,
> a mind to know you,
> a heart to seek you,
> a wisdom to find you,
> conduct pleasing to you,
> faithful perseverance in waiting for you,
> and a hope of finally embracing you.[5]

Aquinas didn't just delight in ideas; he delighted in his Lord. For people like Thomas Aquinas, reason is an aid to knowing God better, not a means for puffing oneself up (see 1 Corinthians 8:1). Those of us who love the life of the mind should avoid the temptation of allowing that love to spoil into idolatry, where our discipleship looks less Jesus and more like the Greek philosophers in Athens who loved nothing other than "talking about and listening to the latest ideas" (Acts 17:21).

The Beginning of the Christian Mind

The purpose of this book is to encourage disciples to love God with all their minds. We believe this is applicable for anyone committed to following and learning from Jesus as disciples. So where do we start? Where does loving God with our minds begin?

The author James Sire argued that the Christian mind begins with an attitude.[6] It begins in humility and reverent fear of God. The Scriptures support this idea. The first chapter of Proverbs tells us that "the fear of the Lord is the beginning of knowledge, but fools despise wisdom and instruction" (Proverbs 1:7). The prophet Isaiah reflects this same need for humility and reverence when it comes to knowledge:

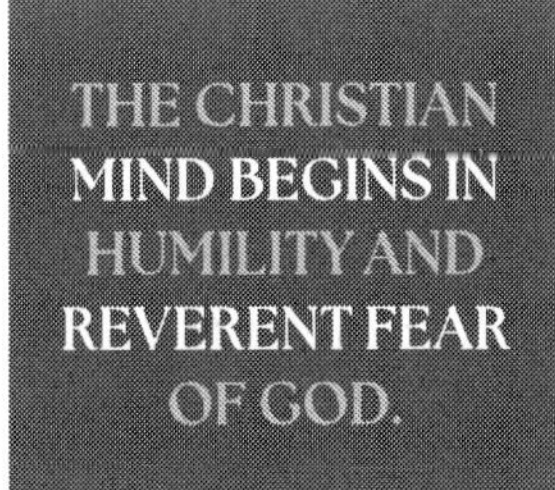

> "For my thoughts are not your thoughts,
> neither are your ways my ways,"
> declares the Lord.
> "As the heavens are higher than the earth,
> so are my ways higher than your ways
> and my thoughts than your thoughts."
> (Isaiah 55:8–9)

The Christian mind joins David as he is lying in a field on a still night, looking at the star-filled sky and proclaiming the greatness of the God:

> LORD, our Lord,
> how majestic is your name in all the earth!
> You have set your glory
> in the heavens.
> Through the praise of children and infants
> you have established a stronghold against
> your enemies,
> to silence the foe and the avenger.
> When I consider your heavens,
> the work of your fingers,
> the moon and the stars,
> which you have set in place,
> what is mankind that you are mindful of them,
> human beings that you care for them?
> (Psalms 8:1–4)

It is only reasonable that loving God with our minds would begin with an attitude of humility. After all, God is the Creator of all things, including our minds. Our capacity for thought is a gift from God. In fact, many people have reasoned quite persuasively that our capacity for rational thought is one of the best arguments for the existence of God.

A foolish person looks down on the God of the universe from the ridiculous perch of his own limited knowledge. Instead of directing his mind toward God with a faith seeking understanding, the fool shrinks God to fit within the cramped confines of his own mind. A wise person, however, knows who he is in relationship to God. By pairing the discipleship of the mind with a vibrant practice of prayer and worship, believers can find the humility and reverence that mark the beginning of wisdom.

If loving God with our minds begins with an attitude, where does it end? In other words, what is the goal of the Christian mind? We suggest that the destination of the Christian mind is Jesus. By this we mean that a Christian mind thinks *about* Jesus, *like* Jesus, and *through* Jesus.

Thinking About Jesus

Our thoughts have a unique ability that almost nothing else has. Our thoughts can be about other things. We don't just think. We think *about* things. We don't just have beliefs. We have beliefs *about* things. A guitar can't be *about* anything. Neither can a car or a pencil. A book or a film can be about something only because those things reflect the "aboutness" of the thoughts of their creators.

The Christian mind is about Jesus insofar as it is directed toward him. We are not saying that Jesus is all we think about; surely there are hundreds, if not thousands, of different things that occupy our minds daily. However, the Christian mind is drawn into intentional seasons of contemplating Jesus. To love God with our whole mind means we cultivate our inner lives, tuning out the constant buzz of distractions and directing our minds toward our Creator and Savior.

One of the biggest challenges to the Christian mind is the busyness that crowds out any moment of quiet reflection. Thinking about Jesus is more than just quiet contemplation, however. Thinking about Jesus also means reading, studying, and reflecting on content that will help us to know Jesus better. This presents another challenge to the Christian mind. Reflect on the content you consume—visual, written, or audio. How much of that content directs you to Jesus?

Thinking Like Jesus

The Christian mind also thinks *like* Jesus. This is at the heart of Paul's encouragement to the Philippians to "have the same mindset as Christ Jesus" (Philippians 2:5b). To be a disciple of Jesus is to daily learn to think like Jesus. We think like Jesus when we think about the nature of the kingdom, about other people, about sin and righteousness, and about hope. We delight in the things he delights in. We grieve over the things that grieve him. Having this mindset translates into action. Thinking like Jesus leads to acting like Jesus in radical humility and sacrifice (Philippians 2:6–11).

We are aided in developing the mind of Jesus by the Holy Spirit dwelling within us (see 1 Corinthians 2:16), but this is not an "all at once" sort of thing. Over time, we come to think like those we imitate. Imitate a friend, a teacher, a parent, or a celebrity for a long time, and eventually your way of thinking will reflect theirs. In the same way, if we continue to learn from Jesus and imitate him, we will eventually find ourselves thinking like him.

> WHEN WE IMITATE JESUS, WE WILL EVENTUALLY FIND OURSELVES THINKING LIKE HIM.

Scholar Alan Jacobs offers this wisdom in his book *How to Think*: "What is needed for the life of thinking is hope:

hope of knowing more, understanding more, being more than we currently are."[7] We could add this note to Jacobs's observation: what is needed for the life of Christian thinking is the hope of becoming more like Jesus in every way.

Thinking Through Jesus

Lastly, the Christian mind thinks *through* Jesus. After his resurrection, Jesus told his disciples that all authority on heaven and earth had been given to him (Matthew 28:18). One clear implication of that authority is that we go into all the world and make disciples. Another implication is that we see our world and our culture through the lens of that authority. This helps us understand Paul's words in 2 Corinthians 10:5: "We demolish arguments and every pretension that sets itself up against the knowledge of God, and we take captive every thought to make it obedient to Christ." Loving God with all our minds means that we are discerning; we shine the light of the truth of Jesus on what the world claims is true. Thinking *through* Jesus means viewing our thoughts through the lens of the lordship of Jesus. Whether a belief is culturally popular or personally attractive isn't what matters; what matters is whether it fits with our knowledge of God through Scripture or sets itself up against that knowledge.

We shouldn't be surprised, then, when the Christian mind comes into conflict with the thinking of the world. The Christian mind is a perturbing force in the world. Often that perturbation manifests as a creative influence bringing Christ-centered truth to places where that truth is unknown. Where there is no love, we bring love. Where there is no hope, we bring hope. Where there is no sign of righteousness, we bring righteousness.

There are other times when that perturbing force must be destructive. Sometimes arguments and pretentions must be demolished, and false ideas must be subjected to the truth of Jesus. Writing over a century ago, theologian J. Gresham Machen put our task in blunt terms:

> False ideas are the greatest obstacles to the reception of the gospel. We may preach with all the fervor of a reformer and yet succeed only in winning a straggler here and there, if we permit the whole collective thought of the nation or of the world to be controlled by ideas which, by the resistless force of logic, prevent Christianity from being regarded as anything more than a harmless delusion. Under such circumstances, what God desires us to do is to destroy the obstacle at its root.[8]

This destruction should be done in the spirit of Christ and by the power of Christ. Remember Paul's words in 2 Corinthians 10:3–4: we don't fight the way the world fights or with the weapons the world uses. The Christian mind is noted for its "gentleness and respect" (see 1 Peter 3:15). However, gentleness and respect should not be confused with passivity or disengagement. Thinking *through* Jesus won't allow that approach.

Why This Matters

In this chapter, we have identified three mistakes that Christians sometimes make regarding their minds, and we have also discussed where loving God with all our minds begins and ends. Now more than ever, this is a critical topic for disciples to explore. We live in times of chronic confusion and information overload, times of bitter ideological polarization. We live in times where truth is treated as myth while every fanciful whim is loudly put forth for serious discussion in the public square.

All this noise masks a deeper reality—that we live in times of great emptiness. J. P. Moreland identifies seven characteristics of an empty self, stating that an empty self is inordinately individualistic, infantile, narcissistic, passive, sensate (only believing in the reality of the physical universe), overly busy, and lacking an interior life.[9] Based on this list, we can see signs of emptiness all around us. Did that list also have the uncomfortable ring of personal familiarity? Do any of these characteristics hit a little too close to home?

Each one of us—yes, even those of us trying to faithfully follow Jesus—faces the risk of becoming empty. To combat this danger, we need the discipline of learning to love God with all our minds.

Think It Through

Many of us come from towns or cities where high school football is an important pillar of the community. How might a football game give us an opportunity to think *about* Jesus? How could we think *like* Jesus about football? Lastly, how can we think about a high school football game *through* the lens of Jesus? Be careful with these last two questions. We all tend to project our own biases and assumptions onto Jesus. Be wary when you conveniently find that Jesus tends to think exactly like you do. It might be wise to challenge your immediate answers to these questions.

FOR REFLECTION AND DISCUSSION

1. What are some obstacles that get in the way of loving God with our minds? Make it personal. Can you think of any strategies or disciplines that might help you overcome these obstacles?

2. We talked about the dangers of neglecting, disconnecting, and idolizing the mind. Do you agree that these are dangers for disciples of Jesus? Do you personally struggle with any of these tendencies?

3. Define the "fear of the Lord." What happens if this isn't our starting point for the pursuit of wisdom?

4. Take a moment this week to go on an hour-long walk without a phone or any other distractions. Pick a question about something that matters deeply—a question that needs time and focus in order to think through, such as, "What have you learned recently about being a better friend, parent, or spouse?" During the walk, give yourself the space to wrestle with this question. Reflect on what you learned from the experience.

Captured by Bad Ideas

A long time ago, after the great war in heaven and the angel Satan's rebellion against God, Satan and his demons were cast to the earth, sulking and cursing and licking their wounds. They had lost.

But Satan wasn't done. His anger rose, his contorted face twisting in a hateful grimacing grin. "This is only the beginning," he promised. True, they would no longer be able to plan a direct assault against heaven, but that was okay. They would simply refocus their evil efforts down here.

After all, this place—earth—was the site of God's special attention. God had created this beautiful planet and then placed humans in charge as a kind of steward over his creation. God had created humans with himself in mind; he had created them in his image. And since it was obvious that God loved these humans, it was obvious to Satan what his new strategy was to be. If Satan and his demons were able to somehow hurt these humans—wound them, curse them, or even get them to curse God—then Satan would be hurting, wounding, and punishing God. Revenge.

The question of how best to attack humans was so pressing that Satan called a meeting of his demons.

"My fellow demons, as we have learned, God is impossible to beat." In answer to this came hisses and curses and spits of venom. "Why can't we beat him?" continued Satan. "It's because of his great power."

"However," Satan whispered through a growing smirk, "God is not impossible to wound." The demons grew quiet, wondering what Satan meant. "God may be impossible to beat, but no, he is not impossible to wound. Why? Because of his great love! And though God might be invincible, those he loves are not. Thus, we will wound the Father by going after his children!" This was met with approving roars, sinister sneers, and gleeful growls.

"What we need, my fellow enemies of God, is a temptation. A temptation so effective that it will curse humans for millennia. A temptation so harmless looking that humans will see it as only sensible."

"As you know," he continued, "God has infused this planet with many of his characteristics, like wisdom, love, and kindness. And I believe," Satan said, "that we can use these characteristics—these parts of himself that God has infused into this world. We can take hold of these things and tear them apart. And when we tear them apart from each other, I believe we can create the master temptation! So rip them apart! See what you come up with. Create for me the master temptation!"

With a revengeful roar, the demons got to work. God had infused so much of his nature into his creation that things to use were everywhere. Knowledge had been attached to love, so one demon decided to rip them apart and keep knowledge. He then discovered that knowledge without love was arrogance.

Love had been attached to fairness. So another demon decided to tear love and fairness apart, discovering that love without fairness was favoritism.

That left fairness, which was attached to virtue. A third demon ripped virtue off from fairness and discovered that fairness without virtue was envy. (Envy was soon used to tempt the first human offspring to turn on his brother. The result was a new sin called murder.)

A fourth demon had watched the other demon rip virtue off from fairness, and he decided to pick up virtue, but it was attached to power. So he ripped virtue and power in two, let power fall to the ground, and discovered that virtue without power was self-righteousness.

Another demon saw romance and wondered what he might do with it. But romance was attached to loyalty. He tore them apart and realized that romance minus loyalty was adultery.

Another demon picked up loyalty and saw that it was attached to wisdom. And when he tore wisdom off, he discovered that loyalty without wisdom was folly.

Wisdom might be good for something, thought another demon. He picked up wisdom and found it was attached to kindness. He separated them and discovered that wisdom without kindness made cruelty.

Another demon thought he might be able to do something with kindness, but kindness was attached to truth. *What would happen if I detached truth from kindness?* And he discovered that kindness without truth made indifference. Truth dropped to the floor.

As the rest of the demons were off experimenting with their new temptations, a smaller, timid demon finally stepped forward to see what he could find.

There on the ground were two pieces remaining, unused. They were power and truth. Since neither had been claimed, he picked both up and started experimenting with them.

He tried truth without power, but it didn't create anything new. Truth was powerful all on its own. Then he tried power without truth: pure power, pure intimidation, might makes right. It was so hideous he couldn't imagine anyone ever being tempted by that.

The demon realized with disappointment that truth without power and power without truth didn't really work as temptations, so he just set one on the other and started to walk away. But then he turned back, noticing something about what he had just done. He had placed power on top of truth. He wondered, *What happens when power is over truth, twisting truth?*

So he went back, and with power still over truth, he started twisting truth. And as he did so, power got bigger and bigger. He realized he was on the verge of creating something significant. He envisioned ways in which power could twist truth to get more power—twisting truth about God and twisting truth about people. He imagined the kinds of lies that could be told—lies to beat other people down, lies to wound people—all so that someone could get more power. "I shall call it 'slander,'" he said.

Then he had another thought: *What if I were to twist the truth the other way?* So he started to twist the truth again, and he watched with astonishment as power just kept growing. This time, instead of lies that beat people down, he envisioned lies to make other people feel good. "I shall call these lies 'flattery,'" he said.

The demon congratulated himself, for by putting power over truth, and then using power to twist the truth, he had discovered *two* sins. There was "slander," lies that give more power by tearing people down, and "flattery," lies that give more power by puffing people up.

The time came for the demons to present their new temptations to Satan. One by one, he commended them, "Adultery? Looks promising." "Cruelty! Well done." "Favoritism—we can use that." But nothing was quite suitable for the master temptation; that is, until the end of the line, when the final demon introduced his two new temptations: slander and flattery. Power twisting the truth to get more power.

As the demon demonstrated how they worked, Satan's eyes lit up. "I could *flatter* the humans by making up *slander* against God. Perfect!" Satan said. "I know exactly what I shall do."

So Satan took the two new temptations, shape-shifted into a beautiful serpent, and slithered away to try them out on the humans.

* * *

Ever since Genesis 3, we humans have lived in the haze of Satan's slanderous lies about God. Ever since Satan said, "Did God really say?" and, "You will not certainly die," we've had trouble knowing up from down, good from evil, and the shepherd's pasture from the lion's den. Satan flattered us and slandered God, and the result has been moral, intellectual, and physical chaos in which we see ourselves as gods, the enemy as fun and fascinating, and the true God as a threat to freedom. In this haze, we're at serious risk of being further deceived.

In Colossians 2:8, Paul warns his audience about those who would take them captive through "hollow and deceptive philosophy." These ideas weren't grounded in the truth of Christ. Instead, they were built on human tradition and the "elemental spiritual forces of this world." This philosophy was hollow because it denied the sufficiency of Jesus in whom "all the fullness of the Deity lives in bodily form" (Colossians 2:9) and who has decisively triumphed over the spiritual powers and authorities of this world (Colossians 2:15). It was deceptive because, despite its emptiness, it still possessed the appearance of righteousness and wisdom (Colossians 2:23).

We're not too different from our ancient brothers and sisters in Colossae. The specific nature of the philosophies putting us at risk might be a bit different than those faced by Paul's first-century audience, but there is no doubt that a Christian in our world today remains at risk of being taken captive by empty and deceptive ideas. Our world is filled to the brim with ideas masquerading as wisdom which, once we grant them power, capture us and erode our confidence in the sufficiency of Jesus.

In their book, *Hidden Worldviews*, Steve Wilkens and Mark Sanford point out that most people aren't living their lives from a carefully considered metaphysical system. Most of us—including Christians—are not philosophers. We aren't walking the aisles of the grocery store critically examining our epistemological assumptions while picking up a gallon of milk and a carton of eggs. No, most people are too busy and too, well, *normal* for all of that.

However, this doesn't mean that we live our lives free of philosophical systems. Every one of us has assumptions about the way the world works and our place within it. Thinkers have used various metaphors to describe how this set of assumptions, this worldview, works. Some compare it to a map that orients and guides us through life. Others use the metaphor of glasses that cause us to see the world in a particular way. Wilkens and Sanford compare worldview to a story that we persist in telling ourselves and acting out.

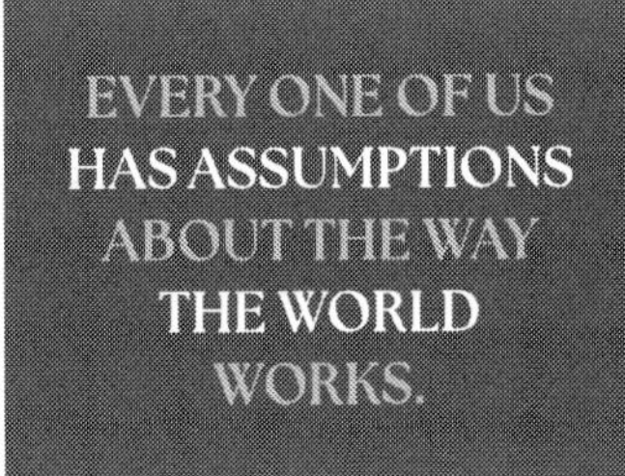

But according to Wilkens and Sanford, we are not always aware of this story:

> The most powerful influences come from worldviews that emerge from culture. They are all around us, but are so deeply embedded in culture that we don't see them. In other words, these worldviews are hidden in plain sight. We will occasionally call them "lived worldviews" because we are more likely to absorb them through cultural contact than adopt them through a rational evaluation of competing theories. These lived worldviews are popular philosophies of life that have few intellectual proponents but vast numbers of practitioners.[10]

In other words, we are highly susceptible to coming under the influence of certain stories without realizing it. Merely by living within a particular culture, we come to adopt hidden worldviews, today's "hollow and deceptive philosophies." These are the ideas that silently creep in and take us captive without us noticing. It's not that we're convinced that these stories are true; it's that we never really gave these philosophies much thought at all. At some point we fell into step with the conventional wisdom of the world and just started assuming it was true. Because these philosophies are hidden from us, we tend to think *from* them rather than merely *with* them. In other words, these become the assumptions that inform and shape the rest of our thinking.

As Christians who are interested in thinking well, we must become aware of the hollow and deceptive philosophies of our day. Wilkens and Sanford identify eight of these hidden worldviews in their book, which is well worth reading. In this chapter, we'll identify four philosophies which are particularly seductive for Christians in our current cultural context.

Apathyism

A life void of thinking deeply about things that matter is an impoverished, sad existence. Socrates found it hard to justify such a life, famously proclaiming during his trial that "the unexamined life is not worth living." Tens of millions of people—including many Christians—are putting that to the test. We have chosen to live lives of unrelenting distraction instead of lives of careful thought and meditation.

Mathematician and philosopher Blaise Pascal, writing nearly four hundred years ago, identified a problem that has only grown worse in this day of omnipresent sounds and screens. In his unfinished work *Pensées*, Pascal observed our tendency to numb ourselves with noise and diversions:

"Being unable to cure death, wretchedness and ignorance, men have decided, in order to be happy, not to think about such things."[11] We would rather settle for the shallowness of endless diversions than become unsettled by contemplation. As it turns out, this numbed existence isn't necessarily a happier one. Living in fear of boredom and quiet leaves us far more unsettled than contemplation would. Pascal concluded rather boldly that "the sole cause of man's unhappiness is that he does not know how to stay quietly in his room."[12]

We call this hollow and deceptive philosophy "apathyism." Unlike with atheism or agnosticism, it's completely possible to believe in God and still be an apathyist. The apathyist may believe in God, but he would rather not think about God. He'd rather not think about much of anything beyond today's diversions. This kind of apathy is not laziness or lethargy; it is often the opposite. Apathyism is active and anxious, rarely slowing down or resting long enough for deep thinking. A disciple living in our always-on, always-connected culture is especially susceptible to this philosophy.

Apathyism is dangerous for the disciple of Jesus because it inevitably leads to stunted spiritual growth. It also lowers our defenses against other toxic ideas pervasive in our world.

Relativism

In 2016, the Barna Group conducted a study on the moral beliefs of Americans across age groups. They discovered that a significant majority of American adults had concerns about the nation's moral condition, but there was less agreement on what constituted morality itself. Nearly 70 percent of adults with no faith believed that morality is whatever is right for one's own life. Around 40 percent of practicing Christians also endorsed this definition of morality. The survey revealed that almost 90 percent of all adults believed that people should not criticize someone else's life choices, and 76 percent of Christians believed the same thing. The majority of Christians, 61 percent, agreed that people can believe whatever they want as long as those beliefs don't affect society. Nearly 80 percent of all adults, regardless of faith, agreed with that statement.[13]

This survey only adds to the mountain of evidence that, regarding truth and goodness, the dominant story of our culture is relativism. Relativism is the belief that each individual or group of individuals determines what is right and true for them. According to relativism, there is no benchmark when it comes to truth; there is only our own perspective. To be fair, there are different shades of relativism, from the extreme relativist who denies all absolute truth to the mild relativist who might simply be uncomfortable with certain claims of truth. Most relativists fall into the second category.

It is a good thing to be humble in our truth claims and honest about what we can and cannot know. The problem is when humility strips us of all conviction and we lose the confidence to stand on anything true. As the saying goes, we become so open-minded that our brains fall out. Relativism takes us captive by turning all of our beliefs into mere personal opinions, private feelings, or vague spiritualties. Applied to Christianity, relativism goes something like this: *Sure, I*

RELATIVISM TURNS OUR BELIEFS INTO PERSONAL OPINIONS, PRIVATE FEELINGS, OR VAGUE SPIRITUALTIES.

believe in Jesus, but my belief is mine alone. Of course people will believe differently than me, and when they do, who am I to tell them they are wrong? Relativism silences us and creates a separation between what we believe in private and how we live in public.

Expressive Individualism

In the 1980s, sociologist Robert Bellah coined the phrase "expressive individualism" to describe a mindset that was taking over contemporary life. Theologian Carl Trueman summarized this mindset in his book *Strange New World*: "In short, the modern self is one where authenticity is achieved by acting outwardly in accordance with one's inward feelings."[14] According to Trueman, with expressive individualism "we do not so much think about the world as we intuitively relate to it."[15] This philosophy is perhaps best captured by the conventional wisdom that tells us that the best path to truth and happiness is to just "follow our hearts." Expressive individualism walks hand in hand with relativism; if there is no absolute truth to be found, then it stands to reason that the only truth that matters is our own. This thinking is so deeply ingrained in our culture that the phrases "my truth" and "your truth" have become cliché.

Disciples who think from a worldview of expressive individualism will struggle to see the importance of saying no to those "sinful desires which wage war against your souls" (1 Peter 2:11). Thinking from this hollow and deceptive philosophy means disciples will struggle to encounter and submit to a Lord who wants us transformed beyond mere authenticity. We are reminded in Jeremiah that "the heart is deceitful above all things" (Jeremiah 17:9a). We are easily deceived when the only person we listen to is ourselves; we will substitute our own voice for heavenly wisdom.

Practical Atheism

The final hollow and deceptive philosophy involves the assumption that God may *exist* but his *presence* can be ignored. This is the lifestyle that James was challenging in James 4. In this worldview, God is an afterthought as someone lives their life and makes their plans. Some people use the word "deism" to describe this philosophy, but practical atheism might be a better description because, in practice, such a person is indistinguishable from an unbeliever. If practical atheists think about God at all, they think about him as a dispassionate observer of their lives who wants them to be happy and hopes that they're generally good. Such a "religion" finds wide acceptance in our culture; it is seen as safe, moderate, and non-judgmental. Nearly twenty years ago, sociologist Christian Smith already saw this worldview, which he labelled "moralistic therapeutic deism," as the dominant belief system of American youths.[16]

Thinking from practical atheism goes beyond treating God as an afterthought in our personal choices. It also fosters skepticism about God's intervention in the world. It biases us against the existence of miracles or answered prayers. It blinds us to the realities of spiritual warfare. Eventually it may degrade our understanding of Scripture and even the incarnation of Jesus. With practical atheism, the idea of God shrinks away to become a mere concept devoid of any power.

In each hollow and deceptive philosophy, we hear echoes of slander against God. In apathyism, God isn't worth caring about. In relativism, God isn't worth listening to. In expressive individualism, God isn't worth obeying. In practical atheism, God isn't worth believing in. The root of Christian worship is believers telling our God that he *is* worthy. A key part of resisting hollow and deceptive philosophies is letting our worship of God mature from a series of isolated inspirational experiences into an integral part of our worldview.

IN EACH DECEPTIVE PHILOSOPHY, WE HEAR ECHOES OF SLANDER AGAINST GOD.

Think It Through

Imagine that your teenage daughter comes home from school one day and tells you that her best friend is making a series of questionable decisions. When you ask your daughter what she plans to do about it, she shrugs and tells you that there's nothing she can do. After all, her friend isn't a Christian, and your daughter is very concerned about being thought of as judgmental. She concludes helplessly, "Who am I to tell her what's right and wrong?" How do you respond to your daughter?

your daughter has a point if the girl isn't a Christian. She can speak truth to her and should, but the real remedy is the gospel. She needs to be born of the Spirit.

FOR REFLECTION AND DISCUSSION

1. In this chapter, we mentioned several hollow and deceptive philosophies. These philosophies may affect the ways we think and act without our even realizing it. Reflecting personally, have you seen any evidence of these philosophies in your own life?

2. Give one example of each of these philosophies that you see in our culture.

3. Are there any additional hollow and deceptive philosophies you've observed that weren't mentioned in the chapter?

4. What is one step you can take to challenge the influence of these philosophies in your life?

Thinking Like a Grown-Up

A body lay lifeless in the kitchen, covered with a blanket. It was the body of the host. Someone whom he had invited to last night's party was guilty of his murder. The police had been called, and now the detective had gathered all the guests in the hearth room. He was going to reveal the murderer.

Once everyone was gathered in the same room, the detective began: "Somebody in this room is guilty of murder. Up until now, only one of you knew who. That *one* was the murderer. But now, two people know who did it: the murderer and me. I'm going to reveal to you the name of the guilty culprit."

Everyone in the room gasped.

"As you probably know, the victim had a vast amount of wealth," said the detective. "At first, that directed my attention to Greed. I thought perhaps he was the culprit." Greed raised his eyebrows. "But when I realized Greed was busy at the poker table during the time of the murder, I realized it was likely someone else."

"Yes, very good," Greed replied. "And how much did you say the victim left behind?"

But the detective had moved on. "Pride," he continued. Pride looked up with an unmistakable air of offense. "You mentioned that this was the *first* time you were invited to the victim's home, that he had hosted numerous get-togethers in the past months, and that you were dumbfounded that this was your first invite. That would give you motive, wouldn't it? To make sure the victim never slighted you again?"

"It was outrageous—outrageous—I tell you! Doesn't he know who I am?" Pride burst out, red-faced.

"But then I learned that you were busy in conversation with Ignorance at the time of the murder, rattling off a list of your accomplishments."

"Pride has done so many great things!" added Ignorance. "You really should hear it for yourself, detective. It's truly fascinating."

"Maybe some other time," the detective replied. Then he continued, "Next I thought about Envy. This is your eighth time to be invited here, isn't it, Envy?"

"Yes," Envy muttered. "What about it?"

"As I interviewed the people who know you, the same theme kept recurring. They told me you've always got something covetous to say about this place. The size of the chandeliers, the elegance of the rugs, the privilege of the people in the portraits. Isn't it true that you told Greed you would *kill* for a house like this?"

"It was just a metaphor," Envy retorted, looking up at the detective bitterly.

"A meta-what?" asked Ignorance. Everyone ignored the question.

Greed spoke up: "To be clear, I remember advising Envy that there are far better ways to get what you want than killing. Just to be clear."

The detective continued, "It's been confirmed that Envy was over there eyeing those curtains at the time of the murder. I've also learned that, during the murder, Sloth was sitting on that chair, next to Drunkenness. They were both drinking, completely unaware of what was happening." Sloth, who was slouching in a chair, only responded to this by following the detective with his eyes. Drunkenness continued holding his head in his hands. He looked like he was about to break into a confession until it became clear that he was just nursing a headache.

"So I ask you, ladies and gentlemen: Whom does that leave?" the detective asked.

The guests began looking around. Some used their fingers to point and count. Within seconds, it became clear that everyone there had already been mentioned. The detective had mentioned everybody present—and everyone seemed to be cleared.

Ignorance's eyes got wide. He asked the detective, "Did—did *you* do it? Are you going to murder us *too*?!"

"Oh, shut up, Ignorance," said Pride. "Nobody cares what you think."

"And *that*," the detective continued, "is why it took us so long to arrive at our culprit. The investigation showed that the victim's wine glass contained poison. Guess who was in the kitchen just a few minutes before the victim was poisoned?"

"Who?" asked Ignorance, again wide-eyed.

The detective finally revealed his conclusion" "None other than . . . Ignorance! You were playing a prank on the victim, weren't you, Ignorance?"

"Yeeesss," Ignorance nodded slowly. "I was spiking our host's wine glass with salt. Why are you asking me this?"

"Because," continued the detective, "that was not salt. That was . . . cyanide."

"Cya-what?" Ignorance asked, clueless. And it occurred to the detective that *everybody* in the room now knew who the murderer was, except for one person: the murderer.

As it turns out, ignorance can be just as dangerous as any vice.

* * *

The Corinthian church of the first century wasn't known for its maturity. The believers there struggled with divisiveness, sexual license, disorganized worship, and the misappropriation of spiritual gifts. They even had a skewed view of the resurrection. Paul told the Corinthians that they were still worldly and immature. In his words, they still needed "milk" instead of the solid food of adulthood (1 Corinthians 3:2).

Apparently, a major cause for the Corinthians' immaturity was their thinking. Three different times in his first letter to them, Paul uses the word "mature" (*teleios* in Greek) to challenge the Corinthians to grow out of a childish mindset. In 1 Corinthians 14:20, *teleios* is translated as "adults": "Brothers and sisters, stop thinking like children. In regard to evil be infants, but in your thinking be adults." Note the contrast—when it comes to evil, it's good to be innocent as opposed to experienced. Thinking, on the other hand, requires the sophistication that comes with maturity, something very close to what we could call wisdom. Yet how often do we get these reversed? We become sophisticated in evil while eschewing wisdom like a toddler refusing his vegetables, leaving our thinking underdeveloped and naïve. This is truly dangerous territory for any committed disciple.

Discipleship of the mind requires that we take Paul's admonition to the Corinthian Christians seriously. Unfortunately, the wind is not at our backs in the pursuit of maturity. Everywhere we look in modern culture, we see childish thinking incentivized and normalized. It's ironic that in this information age, with supercomputers in every pocket, our culture has become almost unbearably silly. It's clear that information doesn't equate to knowledge and knowledge doesn't equate to wisdom.

A mature disciple works to identify and overcome childish thinking. In the previous chapter, we warned about *thinking from* certain hollow and deceptive philosophies. In this chapter, we warn about *thinking with* certain habits. These habits, or means of thinking, are more characteristic of childish thinking than mature thinking. In fact, these habits are often a way for us to *avoid* thinking. They are impatient shortcuts adopted to avoid complexity or messiness. We assume these tools will make our thinking easier, but in reality they leave our thinking underdeveloped and immature.

A MATURE DISCIPLE WORKS TO IDENTIFY AND OVERCOME CHILDISH THINKING.

Thinking with Pliers

A good set of pliers is one of the most essential tools in any toolbox. Pliers come in all shapes and sizes and can be used in any number of different household tasks. They are best used for securely getting hold of things and then bending, twisting, and turning them in the direction we need them to go. Unfortunately, this function also describes one of our most common habits in thinking. We tend to bend, twist, and turn information so it fits with our preconceived ideas. By thinking with confirmation bias or motivated reasoning, we see only what we want to see and hear only what we want to hear. As social psychologist Jonathan Haidt has said, our convictions have great power to bind and blind us.[17]

How many times have we watched a ball game where the performance of the referees is dependent on whether our team is winning? If our team is up, the refs are doing a great job. If our team is down, we ponder conspiracies about crooked officials. Or what about your favorite politician or political party? Do you ever find yourself explaining away unfavorable stories or choosing only to believe stories that throw positive light on your politics? This is what thinking with pliers looks like. Social media is designed to be a set of pliers, which is why social media often makes us more childish in our thinking. Algorithms that feed us only the news or positions that we like twist our picture of reality while isolating us from people or ideas that might challenge our assumptions.

One area where thinking with pliers is especially troubling is in our reading of Scripture. Rather than letting the text lead, we assert our will over the text. Instead of *under*-standing, we "*over*stand" the text. We bend Scripture to conform to our assumptions and desires, ignoring some verses and twisting others. Such an approach will inevitably lead to stunted growth and immaturity, creating disciples who hear only the echo of their own voice in the text.

Thinking with a Sledgehammer

A sledgehammer isn't a tool of nuance. You don't employ a sledgehammer for delicate work; it's a blunt instrument used to break stuff. Sledgehammers are useful tools because it's often impossible to build something without doing demolition work first. Similarly, mature thinking often needs the destructive force of a sledgehammer. Some ideas need to be demolished and deconstructed. In the previous chapter, we referenced "hollow and deceptive philosophies" (Colossians 2:8), and demolition might be the best way to deal with such philosophies. After all, Paul told us in 2 Corinthians about demolishing "arguments and every pretension that sets itself up against the knowledge of God" (2 Corinthians 10:5a). Sometimes a sledgehammer is the only tool that will get the job done.

The problem is when a sledgehammer is the only tool we know how to use. Demolition and deconstruction have become fashionable ways of thinking among many Christians. Some have aimed their sledgehammer at any idea that exists "out in the world." Any belief that isn't explicitly Christian or any idea that isn't explicitly from a particular branch of the Christian family tree must be broken down and destroyed—often in a very public way. There is no nuance. There is no attempt to understand. There is no inclination to build something positive. There is only demolishing that which we are against.

Others have taken the sledgehammer to key elements of the faith itself, demolishing and deconstructing Christianity down to rubble. Many cease to even call themselves Christians at the end of their deconstruction. Sledgehammers have their uses, but we are thinking childishly when we wield them to destroy what is good and true—and when all we do is destroy and never build.

WE ARE THINKING CHILDISHLY WHEN ALL WE DO IS DESTROY.

Thinking with a Paintbrush

I like painting. It's one of the few household jobs in which I feel reasonably confident. A new coat of paint can completely transform a space. It can also cover up a lot of blemishes. *Thinking* with a paintbrush, however, may lead us to broadly dismiss, mischaracterize, or cover up challenging ideas with a quick brushstroke—especially when those ideas come from people with whom we are already inclined to disagree.

In his book *How to Think*, Alan Jacobs laments our hyper-polarized culture characterized by "willful incomprehension [and] toxic suspicion."[18] Jacobs describes how we identify "repugnant cultural others," which enables us to dismiss and demean any idea coming from a member of this group. We populate our list of repugnant cultural others in all sorts of creative ways. They might be members of another political party. They might live in a different part of the country or world. They might have a different educational or financial status or a different religious tradition. The point is that they are a part of an "out group," which allows us to paint over both their existence and their ideas. No matter what they say, they are automatically wrong.

Politicians are experts with the paintbrush, but most of us have become comfortable with the paintbrush too. However, mature thinkers resist the fleeting enjoyment that sometimes comes with painting in broad brushstrokes. Instead, they engage fairly with ideas and with people who might make them uncomfortable without resorting to bad-faith generalizations and mischaracterizations.

Thinking with a Wallet Ninja®

The Wallet Ninja® is the world's first 100-percent-flat multitool with eighteen tools in one! Can you believe it? Forget the printing press: *this* is the height of human accomplishment. We've all seen breathless advertisements like these for the latest wonder tool guaranteed to change our lives for a low, low price. It's no accident that these advertisements usually catch us lounging on our couches watching TV. Being in a relaxed, sedentary state makes us especially prone to purchasing the latest innovation to make our lives even easier. Some of these tools are genuinely helpful, but others make a lot of promises only to end up discarded and forgotten in some kitchen junk drawer. Tools like this are not serious; they're gimmicks.

Just as we should be wise about the latest overhyped innovation, mature thinkers should also be wise about chasing every novel idea. Wisdom tells us that new doesn't necessarily equal true. The converse is also valid, however. While mature thinkers should avoid uncritically accepting every new idea, they should also avoid the mistake of uncritically accepting any idea simply because it's not new. Mature thinkers pursue what is true without shortcuts based on novelty or tradition.

MATURE THINKERS PURSUE TRUTH WITHOUT SHORTCUTS BASED ON NOVELTY OR TRADITION.

Thinking with Tweezers

In Matthew 7, Jesus warned us about focusing on the speck of sawdust in someone else's eye while neglecting the plank in our own. We can apply this warning to our thoughts as well. Hypocrites are skilled at using tweezers: childish thinking insists on seeing every tiny flaw in someone else's thinking while ignoring any flaws in our own. Sometimes this takes the form of a "sunk-cost fallacy" where we refuse to examine an idea or belief because we have personally invested so much into it.

Mature thinkers are open to the reality that, just as all of us have sinned, none of us is infallible in our thinking. We are often wrong, either in total or in part. This is where the thinker needs to possess both humility and courage. As Jesus explained, the first step in pointing out any flaws in others is recognizing our own. It is a good exercise to occasionally reflect on the things about which you have changed your mind through the years. What made you reconsider? What lessons did you learn from the experience of changing your mind, and how can you apply those lessons to your thinking today? As Christians, we need to develop humility in our thinking—toward God first and foremost, but also toward each other.

Think It Through

To think well, we must learn the difference between a "straw man" and a "steel man." A straw man argument is when we intentionally mischaracterize a competing position so it is easier to dismiss. In contrast, the steel man method is when we refuse to argue against a position until we have carefully and faithfully represented it. As an example, consider "gender-confirming care" for transgender individuals. What would be the difference between responding to this controversial topic using a straw man argument versus a steel man argument?

FOR REFLECTION AND DISCUSSION

1. How would you describe the difference between information, knowledge, and wisdom? What gets in the way of moving from information to knowledge to wisdom?

2. Talk about each one of the habits of immature thinking listed in this chapter. Which one of these tools do you tend to use the most?

3. What are some of your "repugnant cultural others"? What is a more Christlike way of engaging with those we are inclined to disagree with?

4. This chapter described some attributes of immature thinking. What are some characteristics of a mature thinker?

The Holy Spirit and the Mind

As she sat in church listening to the sermon, things took a weird turn. The preacher's style was engaging as usual, but today's topic seemed strange.

"So I say, walk by the Spirit, and you will not gratify the desires of the flesh," the preacher quoted from the apostle Paul's letter to the Galatians.

Walking by a Spirit? she thought. The preacher also quoted a verse out of Romans 8 about being "*led* by the Spirit" and another verse from Ephesians on "*living* by the Spirit."

Her thoughts drifted: *That's . . . weird. "Walking by the Spirit" makes it sound like I'm taking orders from above through an earpiece. What about my rights as an individual? Would it even be my life anymore?*

As the preacher kept talking, the churchgoer mulled over the problem. *What would it even look like to walk by a "Spirit"? I mean, I can agree with a lot of the Bible's teachings about right and wrong and being a loving person. But doesn't the idea of "spirits" take us back to a pre-scientific era? Maybe it's meant to be a metaphor. But . . . he doesn't seem to be talking like it's a metaphor. He's a nice guy, but maybe he's not as scientifically literate as I thought a person of his education would be. Well, on the other hand, he did go to a "Bible" college, not exactly a real university.*

When she resumed listening to the preacher, he was describing what a difference it could make in our lives if we were walking by the Spirit. "Just imagine what could happen for our city," he continued, "if our church alone took this Bible passage seriously and began following the Spirit's lead in our homes, our workplaces, and our friendships."

Well, he'd told them to imagine, so she took him up on it. *Honestly, that sounds a little freaky. Maybe a bit cultish? A bunch of Christians robotically walking in step to a guiding voice. Throughout history, whenever Christians banded together to do stuff in a city, wasn't it usually destructive? Maybe driving a Jewish family out of town or burning a scientist at the stake? No thank you. Much better to use our brains than to "walk" by some puppet-master "Spirit."*

The preacher was wrapping his sermon up, and she was already done listening. *I'm so ready for lunch*, she thought. *I wonder what song the band will close with.*

And that is how she dismissed the idea of walking by the Spirit. She did it by continuing to be led by the individualistic, materialistic, anti-Christian, and distracting spirit of the age.

* * *

Paul included a prayer for believers near the beginning of his letter to the Ephesians. The main idea of the prayer is expressed in Ephesians 1:17: "I keep asking that the God of our Lord Jesus Christ, the glorious Father, may give you the Spirit of *wisdom* and *revelation*, so that you may know him better." Paul recognized that these disciples needed to be equipped for the difficult task of following Jesus in a place like Ephesus.

First, they needed wisdom. Various definitions of wisdom have been offered. One common definition is "applied knowledge," but I especially like this definition from theologian Paul Copan: "Wisdom . . . is the skill or craft of living—intellectually, morally, emotionally, spiritually, and creatively—in right relationship to God, human beings, and the world around us."[19] Wisdom is practical and relational in its scope. You know a person is wise when they are living their life in a way that leads to personal and relational flourishing.

Secondly, these Ephesians needed revelation. The word revelation (*apokalypsis*) literally means a disclosure or uncovering. We can think of revelation as discernment, the ability to look beyond the obvious to that which might be obscured. Wisdom entails a skillfully lived life, while revelation involves accurately perceiving reality. Both are needed for faithful disciples whether they live in ancient Ephesus or in our modern world.

What Discipleship of the Mind Requires

Two additional observations from this verse tell us more about what is needed for the discipleship of the mind. First, Paul tells us that the purpose of wisdom and revelation is that we might know God better. The purpose is not principally about knowing the world or the self, nor is it about living a more successful life. First and foremost, growing in wisdom and revelation is for the purpose of growing in our knowledge of God.[20] A disciple who is growing in both wisdom and revelation is also growing more intimately acquainted with their Creator. The discipleship of the mind, then, is a *spiritual* act with *spiritual* outcomes. Like any spiritual act, we shouldn't imagine it existing independent of God's power. Disciples can't pursue holiness by their strength alone. Neither can they pursue wisdom and revelation by their own effort. The discipleship of the mind requires God's strength working in and through us.

DISCIPLESHIP OF THE MIND REQUIRES GOD'S STRENGTH WORKING IN AND THROUGH US.

This leads us to a second critical observation from this verse. Paul doesn't pray merely for wisdom and revelation; he prays for the *Spirit* of wisdom and revelation. The NIV properly capitalizes Spirit in this verse because it undoubtedly is a reference to the Holy Spirit. The kind of thinking that Paul is praying for in this verse is not a naturally occurring phenomenon. It isn't the kind of thinking that comes with simply making a greater effort; it comes through the power and influence of the Holy Spirit.

Those who seek after wisdom should be mindful that sin deceives us into mistaking the foolishness of this world for true wisdom. This deception is at the heart of the warning in James 3:13–16, where James cautions against harboring envy and selfish ambition. The twisted logic of the world tells us that the wise person is the one who pursues their own ambitions and desires as a matter of first importance. James doesn't mince his words. This so-called wisdom is twisted; it's earthly, unspiritual, and even demonic!

The foolishness of the world's wisdom is also a major theme in the first two chapters of 1 Corinthians. Paul wants his readers to know God has upended the supposed wisdom of this world: "God chose the foolish things of the world to shame the wise" (1 Corinthians 1:27a). Paul doesn't want there to be any misunderstanding; he reminds us that our faith rests on God's power, not human wisdom (1 Corinthians 2:5). The wisdom of this age, along with the rulers of this age, is "coming to nothing" (1 Corinthians 2:6).

What the world calls a conventional truth is often just a lie whose sharp edges have been worn down through constant repetition. The problem isn't just "in the world," however. The brokenness of sin has touched each one of us personally. What *we* call wisdom is often proven to be foolishness marred by sin. How many of us have been exposed as fools even as we confidently assert our wisdom (Romans 1:22)? Pursuing wisdom without pursuing God will send us headlong back into our own brokenness.

Something We Can't Fix

Because we cannot obtain true wisdom on our own, the discipleship of the mind is more than a matter of learning to think well. It's a matter of longing for the transforming power of God in our lives. As Christian philosopher James Sire explains,

> Since we find ourselves even at our best to be only broken images of God, we are in a fix we cannot fix. If we are to be fixed, it will be God who fixes us. And he does. But he does this not just by redeeming us

> through the death and resurrection of Jesus but through restoring us into his image.[21]

Remember Paul's exhortation in Romans 12:2. Rather than conforming to the pattern of this world, we are to be transformed by the renewing of our minds. We will not experience transformation unless our minds are renewed. This is dramatic language reflecting a dramatic change.

Sire links the pursuit of a Christian mind to a passion for holiness, a passion for God to remake us, to transform all of us including our minds.[22] We don't long merely to "think better"; we long to have a mind that *knows* Jesus (Ephesians 1:17) and is *like* Jesus, who is the very power and wisdom of God (1 Corinthians 1:24). This kind of change requires an outside power. We don't bring about our own renewal or transformation; these changes happen only at the intersection of God's grace and our surrender.

> OUR TRANSFORMATION HAPPENS AT THE INTERSECTION OF GOD'S GRACE AND OUR SURRENDER.

Understanding by the Spirit

In 1 Corinthians 2, we find an audacious claim: it is only by God's Spirit that anyone can truly have heavenly wisdom and the mind of Christ. A person without the Spirit might know a great many things. But when it comes to wisdom, "the person without the Spirit does not accept the things that come from the Spirit of God but considers them foolishness, and cannot understand them because they are discerned only through the Spirit" (1 Corinthians 2:14). In contrast, disciples of Jesus have received the "Spirit who is from God, so that we may understand what God has freely given us" (1 Corinthians 2:12). Because we are "in the world" and subject to the brokenness of sin, we need God himself to help us discern the things of God. Imagine entering a culture in which you are unfamiliar with the language or the customs. You might be able to communicate in basic ways, but if you really want to understand and be understood, you need an expert translator. The Holy Spirit functions in a similar way.

God exceeds the capacities of our limited reason. However, this doesn't mean that Christian belief is irrational. God has created us as rational beings to seek out and live by truth. The believer still has need for reason, but reason occupies a secondary place to the Holy Spirit for the disciple. Christian philosopher and apologist William Lane Craig made a helpful distinction in his book *Reasonable Faith*, stating that "although arguments and evidence may be used to support the believer's faith, they are never properly the basis of that faith." According to Craig, the basis of our faith, the way we *know* that Christianity is true, is "the self-authenticating witness of God's Spirit," who lives within every believer (see 1 John 3:24).[23] It's important to grasp this distinction because the consequence of putting reason first is our own rationality becoming the judge of all things. If our rationality is in charge, we'll try to conform an infinite God to our limited human understanding.

REASON OCCUPIES A SECONDARY PLACE TO THE HOLY SPIRIT FOR THE DISCIPLE.

We shouldn't push this passage to say more than it means. For instance, it would be pushing this passage too far to conclude that the unbeliever is incapable of ever coming to know anything about God. Obviously, this isn't the case; otherwise none of us would have ever become believers. God can and does work on the lives of believers and unbelievers alike. The question is the extent to which a person is willing to soften their heart and respond to God in surrender. It is unfortunately often the case that unbelief brings about a hardness of heart which can't be penetrated even by reason. I'm reminded of this quote from prominent atheist philosopher Thomas Nagel who, at the end of a book highlighting many of the problems with atheism, nevertheless concludes:

> I want atheism to be true and am made uneasy by the fact that some of the most intelligent and well-informed people I know are religious believers. It isn't just that I don't believe in God and, naturally, hope that I'm right in my belief. It's that I hope there is no God! I don't want there to be a God; I don't want the universe to be like that. My guess is that this cosmic authority problem is not a rare condition and that it is responsible for much of the scientism and reductionism of our time.[24]

This passage also doesn't mean that the believer has special insight into all subjects. Paul is talking specifically about discerning spiritual truths in this passage; the presence of the Holy Spirit doesn't guarantee the believer a special understanding of quantum mechanics, constitutional law, the nuances of the infield shift in Major League Baseball, or how to swap out the water pump in a Ford truck. But when it comes to knowing God, his Spirit gives us understanding and discernment we otherwise wouldn't have.

Three Steps We Can Take

In this chapter, we have argued that the discipleship of the mind, like any other element of discipleship, requires our submission to the power of the Holy Spirit. Dallas Willard puts it helpfully:

> Our activities must come from within a framework of discipleship in which we are constantly dependent upon the interaction of the Holy Spirit with our souls, one in which we refuse to depend upon our natural abilities and relationships in the world, social as well as physical, "apart from God."[25]

We don't think Christianly apart from God. On a practical level, how can we "depend upon the interaction of the Holy Spirit" in our thoughts? Let's examine three recommendations, all of which require humility and intentionality.

First, as Paul did with the Ephesians, we make this an item of prayer. We confess our need for wisdom and discernment. We repent of our arrogance and recognize the ways that we have been seduced by the wisdom of the world. We ask God to provide us with spiritual clarity in his way and in his time. Thinking well and praying well go hand in hand.

Second, we search the Scriptures for God's truth. God has revealed himself to us in his Spirit-breathed Word, so our search for wisdom should take us again and again to that Word. As we go to God's Word, we go with a posture that is ready to listen and submit.

Third, we recognize that we are not the only ones who are indwelt with the Holy Spirit. We are a part of a body of believers who have received the same Spirit. Therefore, wisdom can be found as we participate in that community by listening, learning, and sharing with each other.

Think It Through

Sometimes people try to prove the truth of a belief by saying, "Well, everybody knows . . ." and then filling in the blank with their claim. Yet declaring that "everybody knows" something is an *assertion*, not an *argument.* Arguments require sound reasoning and evidence. Declaring "everybody knows" is an invitation to stop thinking. A lot of the wisdom of our world falls into the "everybody knows" category. Frequently, what everybody knows today is shown to be foolishness tomorrow. The difference between conventional wisdom and foolishness is often only a matter of time. Can you think of any examples of "wisdom" turning to foolishness?

FOR REFLECTION AND DISCUSSION

1. Read 1 Corinthians 1:18–31. Make two lists. Identify what this passage says about wisdom, then identify what this passage says about foolishness.

2. Why does the discipleship of the mind require the working of the Holy Spirit? Reflect on what it looks like to have a mind guided by the Holy Spirit.

3. Does the presence of the Holy Spirit guarantee that our thinking will be infallible? Why or why not?

4. What are some practical action steps we can take to make us more open to the Holy Spirit's guidance in our thinking?

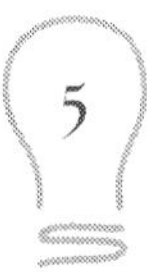

Thinking Well and Living Well

The Devil took him to a high mountain and showed him all the kingdoms of the world and their splendor. "All these I can give you," the Devil explained. "All you have to do is make the correct choice."

He rolled his eyes. This was the Devil, after all. Any choice the Devil offered wasn't going to work out in the listener's favor. "Let me guess," he said, smirking. "I've got to get on my knees and grovel before you? No, thanks."

"Actually, my offer has nothing to do with your body," the Devil said. "It has to do with your mind. In fact, based on the limitations of the human mind, you're going to have to make the choice one way or the other. Do you want to hear the choice?"

"Yeah, whatever."

"Humans," the Devil began, "may have been made in the Enemy's image. You are creative like he is. To some extent, you are free as he is. Nonetheless, your minds are weak. Your minds are easily distracted and corrupted. Take the great poet king whose psalms inspired thousands of generations to worship God. All it took was one lustful gaze to make him forget everything, impregnate a woman, and murder her husband. Your human minds can focus on only one object at a time, and it takes nothing to redirect your focus to where I want it."

"Your point?" So far, the Devil wasn't wrong. It was annoying.

The Devil smiled, sensing progress. "Consider the two great aims of the human mind: intellect and virtue. The true and the good. You cannot hope to pursue both with excellence in one lifetime given your weak human mind. You have to choose. I'm inviting you to make the correct choice between them. If you do, these kingdoms can be yours."

Intellect minus virtue—pursuing knowledge without regard to what evil it might unleash. So the Devil was making him the same offer given to the mythical Dr. Faust. Unlimited space and time to explore, learn, invent, and dominate at the cost of his conscience and at the peril of whoever got in his way.

He imagined with horror the results of choosing intellect without virtue: death, destruction, and misery.

"Have you made your choice?" the Devil asked.

"Not the one *you* would have me make," he muttered, not looking back as he began his descent down the mountain.

To choose *intellect* minus *virtue*? To pursue the true and leave behind the good? Never.

So he set about living a virtuous life: compassion for the suffering, affirmation for the self-doubting, generosity for the underprivileged, and zeal for the oppressed.

At the end of his life, he looked back over everything. How rewarding it would be to see the fruit of his decision to defy the Devil's temptation!

But what he saw surprised him. His compassion for sufferers had led him to unintentionally encourage self-pity and jealousy. The result was that the sufferers became entrenched in their misery and hatred toward people who were more privileged. When their lives didn't get better, some of them were even compelled toward suicide. Could it be that these sufferers were in worse shape than before he had helped them?

His cheerful affirmations had indeed emboldened people to stop doubting themselves and start pursuing their authentic lives. However, he noticed with unease that many of the life paths he had affirmed had led to destructive destinations. His generosity toward the underprivileged was well-intentioned and sometimes helped people. But he had never looked to see whether a person's poverty went deeper than their material situation, so some never found rescue from their deepest problems. His zeal for the cause of justice encouraged victims to turn the tables on their oppressors. The result was complicity in movements which, in the name of justice, discriminated against and even killed thousands of people.

This *couldn't* be the fruit of his choice. After all, he had wisely chosen the path of virtue instead of intellect, the exact opposite of the Devil's invitation.

Or was it?

Death. Destruction. Misery.

They were the result of both paths.

All along, he had chosen the Devil's "correct option"—by making a choice between the two.

* * *

Is it more important for us to live morally or to think well? The answer may seem obvious for disciples of Jesus since we are to be known, above all, for our love (a core virtue in living morally). And yet, settling into this either-or framework likely means our attempts to love well will crash and burn. Think about what happens to a plane that loses one of its wings in midair. The same thing will eventually happen to someone who chooses either virtuous living *or* good thinking. This chapter will explore two interrelated questions:

1. In what ways can we think well (intellect) to help us live morally (virtue)?
2. What are some ways we can live morally (virtue) that will help us think well (intellect)?

Thinking Well to Live Morally

Sometimes the right thing to do is clear. As Jesus put it, "Which of you, if your son asks for bread, will give him a stone? Or if he asks for a fish, will give him a snake?" (Matthew 7:9–10). If you've got a choice between giving your kid a fish sandwich or a five-gallon bucket with a rattlesnake inside, the moral choice is evident.

Other times, the moral choice is not so obvious. Should you help your friend move this Saturday when you're tired from a rough work week? Should you offer advice when your friend is into a TV show you're pretty sure isn't healthy for their soul? Is it okay to take a job promotion that has better hours and benefits but will make you miss Sunday church once a month? Is it okay to tell a lie when your friend asks what you think of their new, unflattering haircut?

When it comes to difficult ethical dilemmas, it's good to pause and reflect. Thinking well can play a big part in making the right decision. Solid ethical reasoning isn't just a matter of your gut-reaction (although moral intuitions can play an important part). Rather, it can involve multiple considerations such as virtues, competing values, divine commands, and fact-gathering. In order to help you navigate these important considerations, we suggest four pairings which will help you arrive at the moral choice.

Rocks and Scissors

Life is full of ethical dilemmas—choices between A and B. It wouldn't be a problem if choice A was taking your grandma flowers and choice B was pushing your grandma out into traffic. That's too easy a choice to be considered a "dilemma." But what happens when both A and B are good things? Do we flip a coin? Not exactly.

The Old Testament gives hundreds of commandments, but throughout the Scriptures we see the divine Author putting those commandments in order. Lying is a sin, but God blessed the Hebrew midwives for lying to Pharaoh—because they were saving lives. God blessed Rahab for the same reason: lying to save lives. And even though followers of God are to be good citizens, Shadrach, Meshach, and Abednego were vindicated for not obeying the government—because they were obeying God.

The Old Testament tells us, "To obey is *better* than sacrifice," (1 Samuel 15:22) and, "How much *better* to get wisdom than gold!" (Proverbs 16:16). We see God tell his people that he cares more about whether they help the poor than whether they impress people with their religious rituals.

In the New Testament, Jesus continues his Father's tradition of ordering our values by saying things like, "How much *more valuable* then is a man than a sheep?" (Matthew 12:12). He tells us that it's *better* to love your enemies than just to love the people who love you. Jesus often healed on the Sabbath, which went against the rules of the rabbis, showing us that it's *more important* to help hurting people than to obey rules about what you can and can't do on a Saturday.

Think of it as a version of rock, paper, scissors in which Jesus shows his disciples how to prioritize his commands. We see another example of this in Matthew 23:23, where Jesus illustrates that certain things are rocks and certain things are scissors:

> Woe to you, teachers of the law and Pharisees, you hypocrites! You give a tenth of your spices—mint, dill and cumin. But you have neglected the more important matters of the law—justice, mercy and faithfulness. You should have practiced the latter, without neglecting the former.

Jesus shows us that righteousness of the heart beats the technical obedience of the Pharisees.

What's at the very top of Jesus' value system? According to him, the rules that beat everything else are to love God with all your being and love your neighbor as you love yourself (Mark 12:29–31).

What was the difference between the Pharisees and Jesus? Was it that the Pharisees cared about rules, but Jesus didn't? No. Was it that the Pharisees cared about difficult rules, but Jesus gave us easy rules? Hardly—read the Sermon on the

Mount. Here's the difference between Jesus and the Pharisees: discerning more important versus less important. Jesus wanted them to stop caring about stuff that doesn't matter and start caring about what does matter. Jesus wanted them, and wants us, to know what was rock and what was scissors.

Bes and Dos

Most of the great ethical thinkers throughout history fall into one of three camps. One camp believes that we determine the right thing to do by cultivating virtue in our lives. They theorize that if we are growing in virtues such as honesty, faithfulness, patience, and compassion, then we're going to be in a better place to choose what's right. This camp's philosophy is often called "virtue ethics" and emphasizes what we are to *be* as virtuous people.

A second camp thinks that, to determine what's right, we need to focus on our duty. By duty, they mean rules that we *ought* to follow, regardless of the consequences. This is often called "deontological ethics." Here's an illustration: Immanuel Kant believed we ought to live in such a way that if our behavior became the standard for all people, it would help and not hurt humanity. So, for example, if I tell a lie, and lying were "universalized," could humans flourish in a world where everybody always told lies? Definitely not. Therefore, I must never lie.

A third camp focuses on consequences, reasoning that we can know the right thing to do by looking at the consequences that follow the decision. If our choice results in good consequences, then it's a good action. If it results in bad consequences, then it's a bad action. Some "consequentialists" narrow their focus to the outcome with the best consequence for themselves ("ethical egoism") or the best consequence for the greatest number of people ("utilitarianism"). These three camps are differentiated by whether they determine if an action is good or bad based on character, commandments, or consequences. But for Christians, making ethical choices is not a matter of "or" but of "and"; the Bible prescribes all three types of ethical reasoning for followers of God.

Character: We are to "be holy because [God] is holy" (1 Peter 1:16) and to allow God's Spirit to grow his fruit in our lives (love, joy, peace, etc.; see Galatians 5:23).

Commandments: Both the Old and New Testaments lay out commands for the people of God. For examples, see the Ten Commandments in Exodus 20:1–17 and Jesus' command to "love one another as I have loved you" in John 13:34–35.

Consequences: Scripture uses this method of ethical reasoning more often than you might imagine. Even some of the Ten Commandments were connected to consequences. The Israelites were not to make idols because God is a "jealous God, punishing the children for the sin of the parents to the third and fourth generation" (Exodus 20:5b). Likewise, the commandments say to "honor your father and your mother *so that* you may live long in the land the LORD your God is giving you" (Exodus 20:12).

If we were to summarize biblical teachings on what makes an action good, we might say something like this:

> We imitate God's character by obeying God's commands, with the result being good consequences.

This is why thinking well about living morally involves *bes* (character) and *dos* (commands) and the consequences that result. Consider these *bes* listed in Romans 12 for followers of Jesus:

- Holy sacrifice (12:1)
- Transformed (12:2)
- Body of Christ (12:5)
- Devoted to one another (12:10)
- Fervent in spirit (12:11)
- Devoted to prayer (12:12)
- Unified and humble (12:16)
- Peaceable (12:18)
- Generous toward enemies (12:20)

Here are some *bes* from just a handful of verses in the first chapter of James:

- Quick to hear (1:19)
- Slow to speak (1:19)
- Slow to anger (1:19)
- Receptive to the Word (1:21)
- Doers of the Word (1:22)
- Compassionate to orphans and widows (1:27)
- Unstained by the world (1:27)

As for *dos*, here's a sampling from just one parable: Jesus' parable of the sheep and the goats in Matthew 25. These represent of the kinds of actions followers of Jesus are to do:

- Feed the hungry
- Give water to the thirsty

- Invite the stranger
- Clothe the unclothed
- Look after the sick
- Visit the prisoner

These *dos* are all connected to good consequences for others and for oneself. Absorbing what the Bible says about who we are to be and what we are to do is key to pairing good thinking with virtuous living.

Facts and Follow-ups

Unfortunately, moral arguments can easily bypass the necessary stage of genuine fact-gathering and jump straight into the hype of finger-pointing and defensiveness. Do you care about doing the right thing? Then care about facts.

Many ethical dilemmas can be resolved by pausing to examine the facts of the situation. For example, take witch hunts throughout history. Thousands of women were burnt at the stake as witches, sometimes because people believed that their alleged black magic was behind disasters such as crop failures. Behind these witch hunts, we can spot two layers of untruths: that the accused women were in league with the Devil *and* that black magic causes crop failure. Witch burnings could and should have been prevented by looking harder at the facts instead of getting caught up in the sensationalism of a witch hunt.

As we consider the morality of a particular choice, we need to pause and gather facts. On the morality of abortion, pause to consider what an ultrasound can teach us about the fetus. On the morality of war, investigate which modern wars have successfully applied "just war theory." On the morality of capital punishment, dig into its application in recent history and assess its fairness.

In addition to gathering facts about the ethical choices, we need to ask what results follow each option. This "follow-up" is the consideration of "consequences" mentioned in the previous section.

A caveat is appropriate here. For the disciple of Jesus, consequences aren't our primary consideration. For example, since the Bible says not to commit adultery, don't waste your intellect ruminating on the ways that committing adultery might play out well in your situation. The command is clear regardless of the consequences. (Incidentally, the Bible is equally clear about the consequences of adultery, and this brings us back to our hunting metaphor. Proverbs 7:22–23 describes the result: "All at once he followed her like an ox going to the slaughter, like a deer stepping into a noose till an arrow pierces his liver, like a bird darting into a snare, little knowing it will cost him his life.")

Yet even though it's not our first consideration, asking where the trail leads does have a place in our ethical reasoning. The book of Proverbs often implores us to pay attention to the path we are traveling, because it always leads somewhere. Regarding theft, Proverbs 1:15 says, "My son, do not go along with them, do not set foot on their paths; for their feet rush into evil, they are swift to shed blood." Regarding anger, Proverbs 22:24–25 says, "Do not make friends with a hot-tempered person, do not associate with one easily angered, or you may learn their ways and get yourself ensnared." Regarding greed, Proverbs 28:22 says, "The stingy are eager to get rich and are unaware that poverty awaits them."

The reasoning in these and numerous other warning passages is that, if a path leads to evil, then avoid it. If you are wrestling with an ethical dilemma, remember that both facts and follow-ups matter.

Salt and Light

Ever since Jesus called his followers the "salt of the earth" and the "light of the world," scholars have debated what exactly he meant by "salt" and "light." Was he referring to salt's quality as a preservative, its pungency, or its preciousness? Light also has numerous theological nuances, such as revealing glory, exposing evil, and illuminating truth, each of which could be why Jesus used it to describe our good deeds. Whatever the exact meaning Jesus attached to salt and light, it's clear from Matthew 5 that Jesus wants us not to lose our distinctive "saltiness," and he wants us to be known for shining his "light" in a dark world.

Part of thinking well in order to live morally involves our distinctiveness as salt *and* our duty to shine light into the world. It's easy for us to focus on preserving our distinctiveness as the people of God *or* shining light into the outside world, but Jesus had *both* in mind for us: not losing our identity *even as* we live as lights in a dark world (see Philippians 2:15). Another way of putting this is that we are to be "in the world" but "not of the world" (see John 17:11, 16). We see an example of this both/and when James 1:27b says that we are to "look after orphans and widows in their distress *and* to keep oneself from being polluted by the world."

We need to be able to stay *who* we are, as salt retains its saltiness, without staying *where* we are, instead going out as light to penetrate the darkness of the world. In the ethical dilemmas you face, make sure you are shining the light of Jesus into the world while keeping your distinctiveness as a follower of Christ. Show grace while staying committed to truth. Empathize with people's hurts while inviting them to wholeness and healing in Jesus. Show hospitality and compassion to the non-Christian while hoping and acting for their ultimate good: reconciliation with the true God.

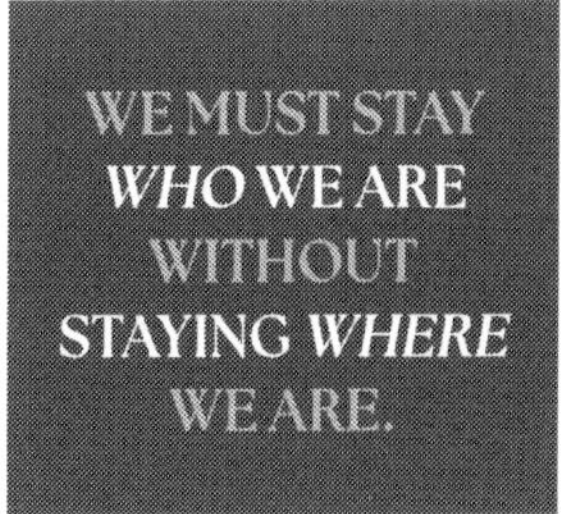

Living Morally to Think Well

Just as thinking well is part of making moral decisions, living morally provides a context for thinking well. In what follows, we offer four pairs of "intellectual virtues" to help you think well. These intellectual virtues all are found at various points in the life of Jesus at the Jerusalem temple; we've included one pair from each Gospel. It's important to think of these in pairs because, as with so many good things, when separated from each other, they can turn into vices.

Humility and Curiosity

The Gospel of Luke tells of an incident that took place when Jesus was twelve years old. Jesus grew up in a family that took the Jewish festivals seriously. One year, while traveling back from Jerusalem after Passover, Joseph and Mary could not find Jesus. At first, they assumed he was with other relatives in the caravan. When Joseph and Mary realized Jesus wasn't with any of them, they went back to Jerusalem to find him. They found their twelve-year-old in the temple, "sitting among the teachers, listening to them and asking them questions" (Luke 2:46). When Jesus' parents asked why he had caused them such worry, he replied, "Didn't you know I had to be in my Father's house?" (Luke 2:49).

The two intellectual virtues we see in this story are Jesus' humility before God, shown by his sense of needing to be in his Father's house, and his curiosity, demonstrated by his listening and asking questions at the temple. These two virtues work together well: humility leads to curiosity, for when we humble ourselves before God, we remember how big he and his world are and how much there is to explore and learn. But when our curiosity is divorced from humility, we get reckless, eventually exploiting people and misusing things. Curiosity minus humility is what happened when Eve and Adam tasted the forbidden fruit from the Tree of Knowledge of Good and Evil. When humility and curiosity are in harmony, the result is a lifetime of fascination and discovery. Working together, these two virtues create soil in which fruitful learning takes root.

Attentiveness and Honesty

The Gospel of John tells of several times Jesus made the trip to the Jerusalem temple as an adult. John 5 records his encounter with a paralyzed man who was waiting beside a pool near the temple, hoping for healing from the waters. In John 8, a group of religious leaders from the temple confronted Jesus with a woman caught in adultery to trap him with an impossible ethical dilemma.

In both stories, Jesus was remarkably attentive to the person in crisis. He saw more than just a paralytic or an adulteress. He saw them as precious individuals who needed his grace and guidance. More than just reading a crowd, Jesus truly *saw* people, and the paralyzed man and the adulterous woman both walked away with newfound wholeness from a grace-filled encounter with him. At another point in his life, Jesus asked a Pharisee who was belittling a woman with a bad reputation, "Do you *see* this woman?" (Luke 7:44). What a profoundly incisive and helpful question. Jesus' attentiveness toward people's needs meant he knew just what they needed to hear.

As an intellectual virtue, attentiveness guides our thinking in ways that are practical, not merely theoretical. Rather than handing down lofty theological hypotheticals, Jesus constantly mobilized his divine intellect for dirt-road problem solving. How? Attentiveness.

Jesus' attentiveness guided another intellectual virtue: honesty. This wasn't the kind of brutal "honesty" that cares nothing about a person's depth of tragedy or level of receptivity. Rather, it was an attentive honesty that earned the right to be heard and specified real solutions. For Jesus, attentiveness wasn't the same as affirmation. Jesus knew that both the formerly paralyzed man and the adulterous woman had deeper issues than immobile limbs and judgmental accusers. He warned both of them about the destructiveness of their own sin (John 5:14; 8:11).

As usual, Jesus wasn't trying to be inspirational or popular; he was being helpful. And being helpful requires honesty fine-tuned by attentiveness. Use these two intellectual virtues to guide your thinking in ways that can change people's lives.

Orderliness and Creativity

To the temple leadership and religious establishment, Jesus was messing everything up: eating with sinners, confronting priests and Pharisees, throwing tables and scattering coins in the temple, and acting like God while pretending to own the place. The leaders mobilized their smartest scholars to debate Jesus, hoping to slash his influence and regain the people's allegiance. The Gospel of Mark records some of their attempted gotcha questions in chapters eleven and twelve: *By whose authority are you doing these things? Should we pay taxes to Caesar or not? If there's a final resurrection, then which guy will a woman be married to if she's been widowed multiple times?* Such questions were crafted to cause a misstep. *Perhaps he'll claim something blasphemous or offend Rome. Or we can punch holes in his teachings on resurrection.*

Each time, Jesus evaded their trap with logical points and memorable interactions. The two intellectual virtues we see in these chapters are orderliness and creativity: Jesus sidestepped the ambushes of religious leaders with answers that were both intelligent and imaginative. For example, he turned the "by whose authority" question on its head by asking where the leaders believed John the Baptist's baptism came from. Jesus knew the religious leaders needed to remain popular with the people, who were fans of John, but he also knew they themselves had rejected John's teachings. Thus, they couldn't answer his question and opted for no comment.

To the question about taxes, Jesus called for a coin, asked whose inscription it bore, and then said, "Give back to Caesar what is Caesar's and to God what is God's" (Mark 12:17).

To the question about the resurrection, Jesus corrected their theology, explaining, "When the dead rise, they will neither marry nor be given in marriage" (Mark 12:25). He also expanded their theology to make room for God's power, reminding them, "God said . . . 'I am the God of Abraham, the God of Isaac, and the God of Jacob.' He is not the God of the dead, but of the living."

The example of Jesus shows us how, if we want to be truly persuasive, we need more than stark syllogisms on the one hand or sensationalism on the other. The intellectual virtues of orderliness *and* creativity combine fact and feeling in ways that can move the needle toward truth for the people listening.

Courage and Compassion

In the Gospel of Matthew, Jesus courageously confronted the persistent unbelief of the religious establishment with a series of eight "woes." He called out the religious leaders for their love of public recognition, their spiritual acting skills, and their obsessing over what's unimportant while forgetting what matters most to God. There's nothing winsome or inspirational about this monologue, which you can read in Matthew 23. Jesus compared the leaders to "whitewashed tombs" and called them "a brood of vipers." Yet he ended with a note of compassion and sorrow because he loved the city and longed for its leaders to come to repentance. "Jerusalem, Jerusalem," he lamented, "you who kill the prophets and stone those sent to you, how often I have longed to gather your children together, as a hen gathers her chicks under her wings, and you were not willing" (Matthew 23:37).

Here, Jesus models two more virtues that need to guide our thinking: courage and compassion. Courage without compassion becomes tactless bravado, even as compassion without courage becomes spineless well-wishing. When our thinking is courageous *and* compassionate, our intellect goes from mirroring the culture around us to making it better.

Swimming Against the Spiral

In the first chapter of his letter to the Romans, Paul paints a bleak picture of the downward spiral of a life without God: Although we knew God, we exchanged his glory for idols. The result was that we gave in to sinful desires, which made our minds depraved. Wrong moral choices led to foolish thinking, which in turn led to more wrong moral decisions.

Disciples of Jesus don't want to get caught in this spiral of futility. We want to swim against it, but how? We allow discipleship into Christlikeness to permeate both our character *and* intellect. We seek to think well in order to live morally, and we seek to live morally in order to think well. For those who have decided to trust and follow Jesus, our lifestyles won't be cleaned up only by moral living or by smart thinking. Following Jesus involves both.

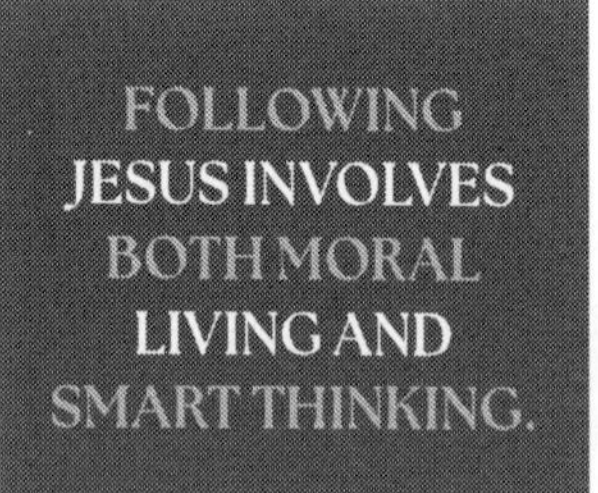

Think It Through

Artificial intelligence is reshaping our world, and continual developments in this field mean that our future will look very different than the present. Because highly disruptive technologies like AI introduce a lot of new opportunities and threats, we tend to receive them with both excitement and trepidation. Yet it is necessary for us to go beyond visceral reactions and *think* about these new technologies. Think about artificial intelligence using the four pairs of intellectual virtues outlined in this chapter. Treat it like a brainstorming session; don't worry about "getting it wrong." The purpose of this exercise is to build thinking habits with virtue as the foundation.

FOR REFLECTION AND DISCUSSION

1. Have you ever thought about how you make hard moral choices? Do you tend to make decisions based on character, commandments, or consequences?

2. Discerning what is important from what is more important can be confusing at times. Talk about a recent situation where you were faced with this question. What should guide us when we face these dilemmas?

3. When we think about being salt and light, what does it mean to stay *who* we are without staying *where* we are? Can you think of any moments in your life when you were faced with the opportunity to be salt and light? How did you respond?

4. Which one of the intellectual virtues comes easiest for you? Which one is the hardest?

The Mind's Grand Story

The convention center was in that chaotic phase of setting up before a conference: banners going up, exhibitors unloading their vans and wheeling merch to their booths, and tables being arranged with books and flyers. Where I sat at the information desk, it was a busy time as people asked for help, wanting to know where to find a certain ballroom or where their booth is located.

Usually, it's easy for me to tell what convention is about to take place. Comic-cons are easy to spot. Tech conferences and trade expos give off their own unique vibes. This convention was more complicated for me to figure out as I watched the booths go up. Each banner had a different "ism": Materialism, Empiricism, Modernism, Utilitarianism, Scientism, Humanism, Feminism, Sophism, etc.

"Excuse me." A man with disheveled hair and a tweed suit was standing at my information desk, peering at me over his round-framed glasses. "Can you point me to the main stage?" he asked.

"Of course," I said and pointed to his left. "Walk down that hallway, take the escalator down one level, and it'll be on your right."

"Are you sure?" he asked, raising an eyebrow.

"Yep, that's where you'll find the main stage," I answered. "Are you speaking on stage today?"

"Debating," he said.

"Oh, interesting. What are you debating?"

He paused and looked around. "It's actually *whom* I'm debating. Empiricism. That's her," he said, pointing to a woman in a multi-colored dress perusing the booths. "And—" he paused and looked around, "—him," he said, nodding to a bespectacled man. Though in conversation with only one other person, the man appeared to be lecturing to a great crowd, with his head raised and hands gesturing. "That's Rationalism."

"And you are?" I asked.

"Skepticism," he answered, narrowing his eyes.

"Say," I began, "what kind of convention is this?"

"This is our annual meeting of humanity's worldviews. Each year, we convene and debate life's most important questions. What is real? How do we know what's true? How do we know if something is good or evil? My area of expertise, as well as that of Empiricism and Rationalism, is how to know what is true." He sighed and half-smirked. "As happens every year, I will win the debate by reducing their positions to naïve absurdity, and yet the masses will continue to blindly side with one or the other. We'll repeat the same process again next year."

"What other debates are happening this year?" I asked.

"As far as main stage debates, there's the ethics debate between Consequentialism, Deontology, and Virtue Ethics. Consequentialism will try to persuade us that we determine what's right based on the consequences. Deontology will try to establish universal duties we must follow regardless of the consequences. And Virtue Ethics will argue for letting virtues guide our actions. Tomorrow, we'll have the ontology debate between Materialism and Idealism. Materialism will argue that reality is physical, and Idealism will argue that reality is the unfolding of ideas. Personally, I'm skeptical whether anybody can know any of these things, but it will be amusing to watch them make their case."

"This is all fascinating," I answered. "When I take my breaks, I'd enjoy watching some of the debates."

"Do you already have a worldview that you subscribe to?" he asked.

"Well, I'm a Christian."

"Oh," he smiled. "I'm sure you won't find Christianity at this convention."

"Why not?" I asked. "Has Christianity never been invited?"

"Years ago," he answered, "Christianity was a regular part of these conventions. But he kept messing the convention up. Annoying everybody. Derailing the debates. Eventually, we came to the consensus that we would no longer invite Christianity."

"So was he winning all the debates?"

"No," he laughed. "Definitely not that."

"Was he not . . . intellectual enough? Was he showing up to the debates unprepared?"

He paused. "Well, no, it wasn't that either."

"Well then, why did Christianity get disinvited?"

Skepticism furrowed his brow, put his hand to his chin, and looked up. "How should I say this?" he began. "Christianity did not ruin our debates by proving us all wrong. No, he did something more annoying than that. He disrupted our debates by showing us ways in which we are all partly right. For example, he kept trying to show me that, while I was often correct to be skeptical of human claims, Rationalism and Empiricism were also correct in pointing us to the general reliability of our reason and senses. He would explain that, because humans are made in the divine image, they can use reason, experience, and even skepticism as tools. And he did that with all our debates. Because God created us in his image, our reality is both physical *and* nonphysical. Because God is good, his character and commands and the consequences that follow *all* play a part in figuring out what's good and evil. It's as if he kept trying to turn our fiery debates into family reunions."

"Well," I said, "I haven't really studied all that philosophy and ethical stuff. But I do know that Jesus tried to bring together people who were enemies. You know, reconciling the tax collector with the Jewish zealot, and that sort of thing. I'm not surprised that Christianity could do the same thing with beliefs."

"But it's all a trick," he retorted. "Sure, it sounds nice. I can still be skeptical about things. Rationalism can still use his reason. Empiricism can still use her sense experience. We can all come together and get along. But it's a trick."

"How so?"

"Because what's bringing us together? What's at the center? It might be the biggest worldview, but it's held together by the narrowest and most dogmatic of all claims."

"And what's that?" I asked.

"That all this is *God's* world," he replied.

* * *

In Chapter 2, we alluded to the trial and death of the philosopher Socrates. Socrates's student Plato, also one of the most influential philosophers in history, narrated his teacher's death in two ways: describing the historical event and creating a parable about it. Plato described how Socrates was put on trial by the Athenians for "impiety" toward the gods and for "corrupting the young." As a teacher, Socrates pointed people toward truth by asking probing questions, and the Athenian officials did not appreciate how he was upending society with his inquisitiveness.

To illustrate his mentor's death, Plato also told a parable, often called the "allegory of the cave." In this story, prisoners were chained from birth inside a cave. All they could see were shadows cast on a wall, and they took these shadows to be reality. One prisoner broke free, made it to the mouth of the cave, and discovered a bigger, brighter world. When he returned to the other prisoners to show them what they were missing, they became annoyed and killed him. This is what the Athenians did to Socrates when he attempted to open their eyes to a bigger world.

Not everybody welcomes the brightness of a world out in the light. Many people don't want their worldview pried open to make room for more of reality. Do you?

We propose three considerations for how disciples can expand their thinking to better match the fullness of reality. We'll need to look at our gravitation toward small worldviews, discuss three goals we need to aim for, and examine three areas for thinking bigger. Plus, we'll find a surprise along the way.

Small Worldviews

A lot of people settle for miniature models of the world. It is as G. K. Chesterton described: "What a little heaven you must inhabit, with angels no bigger than butterflies!"[26] For example, cynics see the world as a charade of smoke and mirrors, while health-and-wealth devotees see it as an infinite playground of swings and slides. Libertines see the world as a place where you can do what you want, while legalists see the world as a place where you can't. Rationalists see a world made intelligible only through the mind, while romanticists see a world made intelligible only through the heart. Totalitarians envision a world under total control, while anarchists envision a world out from under any control. Atheists see a concrete world expunged of all gods, while religious pluralists see multiple "true" worlds ruled by all the gods.

Let's consider the naïve believer in God for whom faith is a golden ticket to a happy life. What happens when they pray for a clean bill of health at the doctor's office—and are met with a frightening prognosis? What happens when, after further faith-filled prayer, the condition only gets worse? One option is that they begin doubting themselves (*I just need more faith!*). Another option is to doubt God (*Is God even there?*). A better option is to realize that their view of the world and its Creator has been too small to match reality.

On the other hand, picture the atheist who reasons that, because the world is so full of senseless suffering, the idea of a good God must be a cruel fiction. What happens when, after making peace with God's nonexistence, the atheist glimpses gifts of grace apparently out of nowhere? What happens when they are confronted with the mystery of a life-permitting universe, a life-permitting planet, and life itself, with all its impossible conditions? Perhaps they begin to reflect on the grandeur of a universe, which they happen to be on the perfect planet to observe,[27] or the miracle of a baby, who can't be reduced to a mere clump of cells in motion, or their own unquenchable thirst to love and be loved, which doesn't reduce to profitability or pleasure.

As it turns out, neither a believer's naïveté nor a skeptic's negativity hold big enough worldviews to fit the fullness of reality. Thinking well isn't merely about navigating the world; it's also about *seeing* the world as it is. It's worth asking whether our worldview has functioned more as binoculars or blinders.

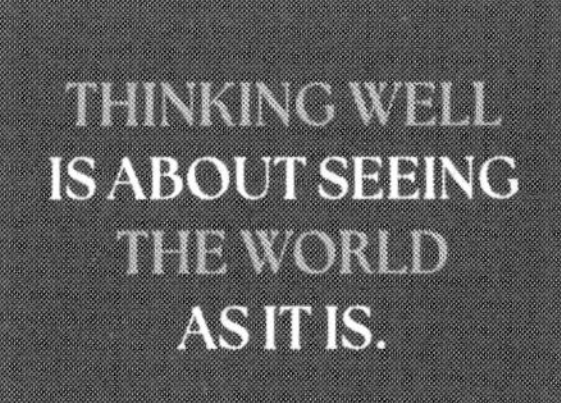

Three Goals for Thinking Better

When it comes to broadening our worldview to fit reality's actual dimensions, there are three goals to keep in mind. First, we want all our beliefs to harmonize with the world as it is. Second, we want each individual belief to harmonize with our other beliefs. Third, we want our beliefs to harmonize with how we truly live. When there isn't this three-part harmony, we'll become irrational and irritable.

It might be helpful to attach each of these goals to its own single term: correspondence, coherence, and pragmatics. If our beliefs harmonize with reality, then they have *correspondence* with reality. If our beliefs harmonize with each other, then they have internal *coherence*. If our beliefs harmonize with how we live, then they have *pragmatic* value, in that they can be practically lived out. All three areas of harmony are fundamental to holding to a true worldview.

Aiming for this three-way harmony also helps us break out of our miniature models of what it means to be a good thinker. A worldview is much more than a list of official beliefs. Being secular or religious doesn't necessarily determine how you truly see the world. For example, you may pay lip service to a church's beliefs while embracing wildly different beliefs in your core. Your worldview is the entire grand story you see yourself in, a narrative that answers your most important questions and gives your life meaning and direction. The most consequential feature of this story is its end—the happy ending that you hope is your destination. This ultimate vision of the blessed life, whether it's heaven or nirvana, the egotistical or the extravagant or the erotic—gives you your cues for the decisions you make.

It's easy to have a worldview too small to accommodate reality, too official to match our core beliefs, or too abstract to integrate into our lifestyle. When it comes to building the question-answering, meaning-giving story by which we run our lives, we need the goal of having our worldview match reality and culminate in an ending that is truly blessed. We'll also want to make sure what we think and how we live harmonizes with this reality-matching view of the world. Again, we want our beliefs to harmonize with reality, with each other, and with how we live.

Three Areas for Thinking Bigger

When considering our worldviews, we need to think bigger when it comes to what is real, what is true, and what is good. For each area, we will look at some tools to help us dive deeper into these categories and arrive at a worldview that matches reality.

What Is Real?

Thinking with a Telescope. A telescope allows astronomers to explore what's "out there." In the same way, part of thinking bigger about what is real is exploring reality to gain a fuller vision of what exists. This is important to get right because our vision of reality frames our dreams and guides our decisions: Is reality just physical or also spiritual? Is reality morally neutral, or do we find good enthralling and evil nauseating? Are humans closer to dust or to the divine? For Jesus, the most important reality was that we have a Father in heaven who loves us, watches over us, and pursues us when we are far from him. Jesus taught that the physical world contained clues to a greater spiritual reality; he brought meaning to the mundane by making parables out of everyday things such as mustard seeds, sheep pens, grapevines, and fish sorting. Thinking through the lens of Jesus will open our eyes to a much wider and more meaningful reality around us.

OUR VISION OF REALITY FRAMES OUR DREAMS AND GUIDES OUR DECISIONS.

Thinking with a Shovel. Another part of thinking about what's real is digging to the foundations of our beliefs. As our shovels dig into the earth, they tell us the thickness and solidity of what's beneath us. After exploring what is "out there," it's important to think through what foundations best explain the fullness of our reality. We experience both goodness and evil, providence and cosmic indifference, the spiritual and the physical, and we can examine which worldview best grounds these experiences. In addition, when thinking through new ideas, we need to dig down and ask where these ideas originate: Is this idea coming from a true worldview or an incomplete one?

What Is True?

Thinking with a Fork. To know whether something is true, break the argument down into bite-sized pieces. Ask if each part is true and whether, when put together, the parts logically lead to the conclusion. False beliefs bind us and keep us down, so we must "take every thought captive" (2 Corinthians 10:5) and examine each one. Many of our problems stem from lies we believe, and that's why we need to wrestle our beliefs into place and determine whether they are accurate. If a belief turns out to be a lie, renounce it and replace it with truth. As Jesus said in John 8:32, the truth will set you free.

Thinking with a Spatula. A spatula is the best tool for flipping a burger or a pancake onto its opposite side. If you want the whole story, don't be afraid to look at the other side of an argument; you might learn the truth more fully as a result. As Christians, we can stay grounded on what God has revealed even as we explore what we can learn from people outside the Christian faith. In Acts 17, we see Paul engaging with both Epicureans (who had an atheistic, pessimistic view of reality) and Stoics (who had a pantheistic, optimistic view of reality). In that discourse, Paul quoted Stoic poets to voice truth about God and humanity. In Acts 23, we also see Paul engaging with Pharisees and Sadducees. Throughout his ministry, he engaged Gentiles, Jews, and Judaizers (people who insisted that to follow Christ, a Gentile also had to obey Jewish law). Paul's example shows us that we need to be open to the glimpses of truth we can learn from other belief systems while using those glimpses to draw people into a fuller picture of the truth.

What Is Good?

Thinking with Rocks and Scissors. As we mentioned in the previous chapter, there are many good values in the world. Part of discovering the right thing to do in a particular situation is learning what are "rocks" and what are "scissors." One of Jesus' most persistent themes was teaching us which values are most important (e.g., saving a life over keeping the Sabbath, inner righteousness over public recognition, showing patience and mercy over passing judgment). We can learn from the example of Jesus to know how to prioritize what is good.

Thinking with a Clamp. Clamps are useful for bringing and holding two things together. Learning to bring together more than one virtue in a given ethical dilemma is a creative and helpful way to choose rightly while adding unity and clarity. We need to hold together truth *and* grace, justice *and* mercy, courage *and* humility, love for God *and* love for people. John 1:14 doesn't depict Jesus as picking grace or truth when the occasion demanded; at all times, he was "full of grace *and* truth."

A Surprise We Find Along the Way

As we seek to build a bigger, reality-sized worldview, sometimes we discover this process to be more complicated than we thought it would be. We get competing messages: Science reveals that our universe and earth are finely tuned for our existence, while often our planet shows the indifference of a massive rock. We experience grace and providence but also gratuitous pain, showers of blessings intermixed with floods and droughts. Rationality and absurdity. Love and loss. Desires both sublime and sinister. Part of thinking hard and well is making room in our worldview for all this fullness of reality, but the learning often feels less like cumulation and more like contradiction.

Along the way, we are surprised to find a way all these contradictory facets of reality can in fact be brought together into a coherent worldview. It's a worldview in which we can see purpose in every pixel.

The truth is that every season, dissimilar as it might be to the others, has its purpose. God's object in placing Adam and Eve in the garden was the same as his object in driving them from it. He pursued Jonah through tugging at a compassion that wasn't there ("Go to the great city of Nineveh" [Jonah 1:2]), then through catastrophe ("the Lord provided a huge fish to swallow Jonah" [Jonah 1:17]), and, failing those, through a series of searching questions when Jonah still wanted vengeance on those God had spared ("Is it right for you to be angry?" [Jonah 4:4]).

God's way of drawing Solomon to himself resembles two half-circles meeting at the circle's end: the path of smart mind ("The fear of the Lord is the beginning of knowledge"

[Proverbs 1:7a]) as well as the path of stupid choices ("Utterly meaningless! Everything is meaningless" [Ecclesiastes 1:2]). In Ecclesiastes, Solomon tells us, "There is a time for everything, and a season for every activity under the heavens" (Ecclesiastes 3:1), and he goes on to list them: a time to be born, to die, to plant, to uproot, and so on. Solomon sees God's hand at work in each moment, writing, "He has made everything beautiful in its time. He has also set eternity in the human heart" (Ecclesiastes 3:1a).

What was God's purpose in waiting so long to come to earth in person through Jesus? Too early, and we might not have known what sin was through the Mosaic Law. We learned how enticing and enslaving sin is through the reign of the Judges and the Jewish monarchy. During Israel's captivity and return, things got tough enough for us to realize how badly we needed God. The story of God's people shows us that childhood instruction, teenage rebellion, and adult regret all have their uses. Able to move about the planet forever would have frozen us in perpetual futility, but a lifetime is mercy, for every stage plays its part in directing us to an open posture. The cross is followed by a gratitude that would not have been there had the cross not been historically preceded by a period of frustration.

Person A wants to be good at getting stuff, pleasure, and applause. Person B wants to be good. God draws both by frustrating them: Person A by allowing him to drink his fill of what turns out to be sand and Person B by granting a few splashes of paradise. The same coin has two separate sides, and God spends whatever it takes on his end. The more time the first man wanders the desert, the more life-saving thirst might bring him to his senses. For the second, the quest for goodness commences at the mouth of a tributary traceable to the sea. Since no one is purely Person A or Person B, it turns out that God draws us simultaneously through our regrettable lusts and righteous loves.

We are messy, and so are the many processes God uses to draw us. Religions neatly trim our duty to enlightening steps or ethical codes, but Jesus turned every town he visited upside down. Like a tornado in a tightly cataloged library, he challenged rules, policies, and motives. Someone once quipped that Jesus was called "Messiah" because he loved cleaning up messes, but don't forget that he caused his share too. Jesus could not boast the clean-cut steps of a Buddha, or the pillared ethics mounted by Muhammad, or the encyclopedic exhaustion of each commandment's implication in Jewish rabbinic literature. If Jesus wanted straightforward, he would have stayed where he was. Coming down, he showed no route to be too roundabout, no person too messy.

Consider utter evil itself, the inner leprosy that drives us from God's presence. For—if we are logical enough to complete the loop—it is our own evil that most effectively drives us back to him. "When he came to his senses, he said, 'How many of my father's hired servants have food to spare, and here I am starving to death! I will set out and go back to my father'" (Luke 15:17–18a).

By facing reality, we are drawn toward trusting God, for stuff rots, pleasure dwindles, and applause deceives. Spending a lifetime getting scammed at every turn makes us pause and listen to the whispers of transcendence. Glimpses of goodness and love weaken our resistance to Jesus, whose goodness makes him impossible not to love. His invitation to trust and follow him resolves the frustrating conflict narrated into every page of our lives. Religions both priest-centered and individualized, projects both geographical and philosophical, pleasures both animalistic and sophisticated—in the end, each hope disappoints. Each promise always breaks as surely as a bubble bursts.

And only one is left standing. The pleasant surprise is that all of reality, in one way or another, draws us to what's real and good and true. It draws us to a story so redemptive that it's literally called the "good news." If the biggest worldview is the one that makes room for all reality, then there's one that does that and more—as it gathers all of reality into a single story and assigns a redemptive function to each role. The biggest worldview is the gospel.

Think It Through

Every worldview tells a story about creation, fall, and redemption. To put it another way, a person's worldview answers fundamental questions about the way the world *should* be, what is wrong with the world, and what is the hope for the world. Additionally, a worldview identifies a person's place in the world. Thus, a person's worldview will reflect beliefs and assumptions about what is meaningful, what is good, and what is beautiful. We are surrounded by competing worldviews every day, particularly in media and entertainment. It's good for us to be mindful of these various worldview messages. Think about the last movie that you saw. How does that movie answer these four worldview questions: How should the world be? What is wrong with the world? What is the hope for the world? What is truly meaningful?

FOR REFLECTION AND DISCUSSION

1. The chapter ended with this statement: "The biggest worldview is the gospel." What is the worldview of the gospel? What does the gospel tell us about the way the world should be, what is wrong with the world, and what the hope is for the world?

Sin has corrupted us as well as everything around us. The hope of the world is the good news of Christ.

2. How does the story of the gospel resolve some of the tensions we experience in our lives?

3. One important test of every worldview is how it looks to live it consistently. Every worldview is pregnant, so to speak, with real-world implications. Based on your answers to the question above, identify several practical implications of the worldview of the gospel.

4. As disciples of Jesus, we should develop the habit of assessing whether our lives consistently reflect the implications of our worldview. Are there areas of your life where your behavior does not match your foundational beliefs? Read the book of James for more about this need for consistency.

How to Think About the World

I squeezed my wife's hand. It might have looked like I was reassuring her, but she and I both knew that I was the one needing courage. We were going on in just a couple of chapters. We had recently arrived in the green room, and I was looking around at the cast of characters.

A friendly, talkative man was telling stories with a handful of other cast members gathered around to listen. He seemed to be in the middle of a fish story. One of them called him "Peter," and suddenly it made sense. This had to be the great apostle Peter, the one who had baptized the first Gentile, Cornelius. That was Acts 11, I recalled. They were now starting chapter sixteen.

I kept scanning the room. Most of the other apostles had left already. A few chairs down from us sat three oddly dressed men, rehearsing their scripts. In another corner, two men were having a heartfelt conversation. The older man appeared to be encouraging the younger, who hung his head and looked sheepish. The older was telling him, "I *know* God has great plans for you, John Mark. Trust me. His grace is greater than our mistakes. Let's stick around. I really think you're going to make another appearance."

"That must be Barnabas," I whispered to my wife, "talking with John Mark. John Mark must still be feeling bad for abandoning Barnabas and Paul on their missionary journey."

"Have you seen Paul yet?" my wife asked.

"He's probably still on set," I replied. "I wonder if that guy ever takes a break!"

Our conversation was interrupted by a friendly voice. "Hi there!" a man said, sticking out his hand. "My name is Apollos."

"Oh, Apollos! Great to finally meet you!" I said, shaking his hand. "My name is Aquila. This is my wife, Priscilla."

"Fantastic," he said. "I thought it might be you. I think we're all three on in a couple chapters. Should we practice our lines?"

"Sounds good," Priscilla answered, but then paused. Some commotion had arisen a few chairs away. It was coming from the three oddly dressed men who had been rehearsing their scripts. Apparently, someone had overheard them and was questioning them about what they were reading.

"I'm not trying to be rude," the questioner explained. "I just have trouble believing you're in the right green room. We're here to participate in the *Bible*."

"We *know*," one of the three insisted. "This is the room the guy told us to come to, and he told us we were going to be in a book called the Bible. That's exactly what he called it."

"But you're clearly studying the wrong script! This doesn't sound at all like the Bible. It's some kind of religious poetry, but it's not ancient Hebrew."

"Again, we *know*," another of the three commented. He looked around at the other two and laughed. "You don't have to tell us what these scripts are. We're the Greek poets who wrote them!"

"Seriously? Let me see that," the questioner said. He reached out, took one of the scripts, and started studying it. "You've got to be kidding. This is about Zeus!" he said with disgust. He began reading aloud, "In every way we have all to do with Zeus, for we are truly his offspring." He handed the script back to the poet with a scowl. "Unbelievable," he muttered.

Suddenly, the door opened, and the room went quiet. All eyes turned toward the man standing in the doorway: bearded and balding, with a furrowed forehead and intense eyes. My wife and I smiled at each other. It was our friend Paul. The room stayed quiet, with all eyes on the legendary missionary-theologian. Even Peter had paused mid-story.

"Epimenides? Aratus?" Paul said as he looked around the room. Two of the three Greek poets raised their hands. "Thanks so much for coming, gentlemen," Paul said. "I'm just getting ready for my speech to the Athenians, and I'm going to need your help convincing them. Would you please step this way?" To the third poet, Paul said, "And you must be Menander. If you don't mind, I need you to hang out in this room a bit longer. I'm going to need you for my first letter to the Corinthians. I've long been a fan of your line, 'Bad company corrupts good morals.'"

As Paul exited with Epimenides and Aratus, the characters in the green room were left scratching their heads. Everyone had noticed how the Bible was rapidly unfolding outward. Each day, some new people group was hearing the gospel for the first time, a new development for a book that had largely centered on one nation. It was starting to become clear why God had placed that nation at the intersection of three continents.

But apparently the unfolding was meant to go both ways. As the gospel blossomed into unreached places, it seemed that some of what was good, true, and beautiful in these cultures would bloom inward. With the Holy Spirit on the loose, perhaps some of these unreached places weren't *entirely* unreached to begin with.

* * *

In the average small, Midwest town, telling someone to "watch out for deer" is a pretty standard way of saying "I love you." You know a person really cares about you if their parting words are a warning about the report they heard from their neighbor whose teenage daughter totaled her car when a scared buck darted in front of her. Love doesn't hesitate to warn you that it's dangerous out there and remind you to be cautious.

This is the way Paul says "I love you" to the Ephesian Christians toward the end of his letter to them. He writes, "Be very careful, then, how you live—not as unwise but as wise, making the most of every opportunity, because the days are evil. Therefore do not be foolish, but understand what the Lord's will is" (Ephesians 5:15–17). Paul doesn't flinch at telling the hard truth. The days are evil. There is no hint of naïve optimism here. Sin and evil are real, and they are pressing realities in our lives. The very next chapter in Ephesians turns our eyes to the battle we've been drafted into, a battle not against flesh and blood but "against the rulers, against the authorities, against the powers of this dark world and against the spiritual forces of evil in the heavenly realms" (Ephesians 6:12). Make no mistake. It's dangerous out there, so watch out. Yes, we follow Jesus and find rest for our souls, but we also follow Jesus into battle.

Why Vigilance Matters

There are several reasons why vigilance matters for the discipleship of the mind. First, we should recognize that the disciple's mind is one of the primary battlefields in which spiritual warfare takes place. First Peter 5:8 says, "Be alert and of sober mind. Your enemy the devil prowls around like a roaring lion looking for someone to devour." When you realize you are being stalked by an enemy, one of the very first things you need to do is think clearly. Our enemy will almost certainly attack you in your thoughts, so don't leave your mind unguarded; be alert and under control. Thinking is spiritual warfare, and neglecting the discipleship of the mind leaves us vulnerable to all sorts of attacks that come by way of the mind. If we have neglected our thinking, then falsehoods introduced as truths can make themselves at home in our minds. We will find ourselves ill-equipped to resist the foolishness that the world calls wisdom, and unaddressed skepticism will start to rot away at the foundation of our faith.

We find another reason alertness matters for the discipleship of the mind in Ephesians 5:16: Paul tells us the days are evil, so we should respond by understanding God's will and living wisely. It might be a bit of a surprise that we live wisely by making the most of every opportunity, even in the midst of danger. Our natural tendency is to seek safety when there's danger; seeking opportunity seems reckless or even foolish. It's hard to imagine a dad telling his daughter, "There's deer out tonight, so make the most of every opportunity." The person who understands God's will, however, recognizes that the Lord has a greater purpose for those who follow him than mere safety.

AS DISCIPLES, WE ARE CALLED TO ENGAGEMENT, NOT HIDING.

As disciples, we are called to engagement, not hiding. A principal way we engage with the world around us and make the most of every opportunity is with our minds. In Chapter 1, we mentioned Paul's words from 2 Corinthians 10:5 about our need to "take captive every thought and make it obedient to Christ." In that chapter, we talked about thinking *through* Jesus, actively seeing the world through the lens of Jesus. Developing a Christian mind involves both defense and offense. We guard our minds because the days are evil, but for the same reason we also engage the world with our minds.

The rest of this chapter is dedicated to exploring this last point—how to engage the world with our minds. A Christian lives in a state of tension—we are citizens of the kingdom of heaven, yet we still live in the kingdoms of this world. The fact that each one of us is embedded in the world makes it difficult for us to recognize all the ways in which we have come to think like the world. (It's always easier to recognize how someone else is being seduced by the culture around them than to recognize the ways we ourselves are being seduced.) We have been called to go into the world as Christ's ambassadors, but we are also called to be holy and distinct.

As disciples of Jesus, it's natural that we love the world with our intentionality (see John 3:16), but loving the world with our infatuation is incredibly dangerous to our discipleship (1 John 2:15).

Wrestling with Complexities in Our World

Our *situation* in the world as disciples creates tensions, but so does our *perception* of the world. Everywhere we look, we can observe a mixture of God's goodness, ever-present brokenness, and hopeful longing. This mixture challenges simplistic thinking about the world. For example, consider the well-known story of Zacchaeus. Most people thought about Zacchaeus in a simple way: "tax collector = bad." That's not how Jesus thought about him. Jesus saw him as *lost* (Luke 19:10). *Lost* is more complex than *bad*. To say something is lost recognizes its value and the hope it will be found. Lost may be a recognition of badness, but it responds with compassion, not hatred or neglect. Add to this the important point that each of us can see a reflection of ourselves in Zacchaeus. He's not some strange curiosity. His story is our story, and each of us should identify personally with his lostness.

We love simplistic thinking. It's easy. It's predictable. It makes us feel like we are in control. However, the story of Zacchaeus illustrates that, when we see the world *like* Jesus and *through* Jesus, we will have to wrestle with all sorts of complexities.

Given these tensions, how do disciples engage the world with their minds? Broadly speaking, Christians have approached the world around them in three ways: accommodation, confrontation, and isolation. An accommodating approach tends to adjust and conform to culture. Accommodation reflects a more positive view of the world. Confrontation, on the other hand, reflects a negative view of the world. A confrontational approach is often hostile toward culture. Whereas accommodation comes alongside culture, confrontation works to change culture through destruction or transformation.

Isolation is another negative approach to culture; rather than fight the world, we isolate ourselves from it. Isolation can take two different forms. Anti-cultural isolation rejects the culture by leaving it in significant ways. Examples of this kind of isolation include groups like the Amish or certain monastic orders. The other form of isolation is countercultural isolation, which doesn't reject culture but instead sees the church as an alternative culture within the world. A Christian counterculture copies something from the world's culture and offers a Christian alternative. This kind of isolation has been common in the evangelical world. We see this quite a bit in art, education, community, and entertainment.

These different approaches to the world are reflected in the figure below:

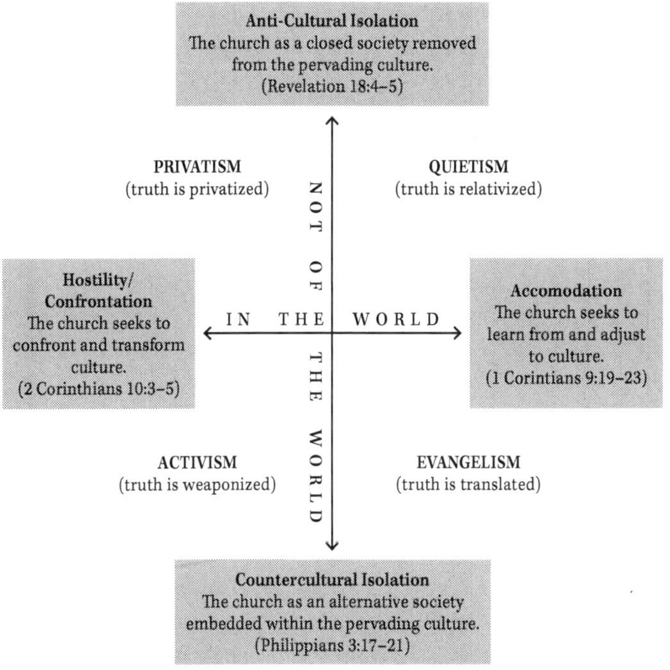

Most of us adopt some sort of balance between being in the world and not of the world. What we call activism, for instance, confronts the world on issues of justice or goodness, but it confronts the world as an outsider, calling people to an alternative way of being in the world. Evangelism differs from activism in that it looks for ways to translate the gospel into the cultures of the world. Evangelism is a kingdom agent who works *within* rather than working *on* the cultures of the world. Quietism is aloof from the world without being antagonistic; it considers the world with all its politics, entertainment, and scandal as none of its business. Privatism, on the other hand, is separate from the world but tends to remain antagonistic toward it. It sees the world as vile and corrupting; so, for its own safety, it removes itself.

Which Approach Is Right?

The approach we take toward the world is one of the areas where Christians disagree with each other most intensely. Naturally, we each think that our approach is correct. We tend to think that other believers who don't have the same approach as we do are wrong, maybe even dangerously wrong.

Take the example of a Christian baker asked to bake a cake for a gay wedding. The accommodator says that the baker should bake the cake. A baker serves all sorts of sinners every day, so why single out the gay couple? Baking the cake might be the best way to love them. The confronter is alarmed by such a compromise. It argues that a committed Christian must fight, take a stand, and make a point, suffering persecution if necessary. The isolationist, on the other hand, might respond that this is what happens when you get tangled up in the world. The isolation viewpoint asserts that it's better to stay disengaged; if you must engage with the world, just mind your own business. Each of these people could probably make a biblical case for their position.

Before deciding whether one approach is the correct one, let's note that most of us are inconsistent in our approach to the world. We regularly change how we interact with the world depending on the context. And often, that's a good thing. In his book *Culture Making*, Andy Crouch identifies four common "gestures" we make toward our culture: condemning, critiquing, consuming, and copying.[28] These gestures roughly approximate the responses we've identified above:

Condemning = Anti-Cultural Isolation
Critiquing = Hostility/Confrontation
Consuming = Accommodation
Copying = Countercultural Isolation

Just as certain physical gestures are appropriate in certain contexts—a head nod or a wave of the hand—each of these gestures can be appropriate at various times. Sometimes isolation from the world is necessary for a Christian. There are some things which a follower of Jesus should completely avoid, and there also are seasons when intentional retreat from the world is necessary for our spiritual vitality. Jesus himself practiced the habit of strategic withdrawal.

There are times when countercultural isolation is necessary. Christian educational institutions, Christian music and entertainment, and Christian hospitals are all examples of Christian counterculture that have blessed Jesus' kingdom and the world.

Certain things in the world demand our hostility and confrontation. The global sex trade and the abortion industry quickly come to mind in this category.

Accommodation can also have its place. We regularly experience God's goodness in the things of the world. A long walk down a mountain trail, dessert at a favorite restaurant, a concert listening to skilled musicians, and countless other experiences can lift our spirits and inspire gratitude. Accommodation can also be an appropriate gesture when we want to better love our neighbors by understanding and speaking their cultural language. Can you truly love your neighbor if you care nothing about the world they live in?

Choosing Our Posture Wisely

The danger is when our gestures become *postures*. According to Crouch, a posture is "our learned but unconscious default position, our natural stance."[29] Accommodation can be fine as a gesture, but as a set posture it leads to weak-kneed conformity to the world. We end up looking, acting, talking, and thinking in ways that are indistinguishable from the world, and holiness becomes impossible. When confrontation is our posture, we will find ourselves constantly looking for reasons to be angry. Rather than blessing the world, we will be known only by the things we are against. Isolation as a posture leads to disengagement and callousness. We may eventually find ourselves adopting an attitude that says, "Who cares what happens to the world? After all, *we're* saved." With a posture of isolation, we risk forgetting that we are no better than unbelievers; we've merely discovered the grace of Jesus.

THE DANGER IS WHEN OUR GESTURES TOWARD THE WORLD BECOME *POSTURES.*

First Peter 2:11–12 challenges each one of these postures:

> Dear friends, I urge you, as foreigners and exiles, to abstain from sinful desires, which wage war against your soul. Live such good lives among the pagans that, though they accuse you of doing wrong, they may see your good deeds and glorify God on the day he visits us.

For the confronters, Peter reminds us to live such good lives that the pagans glorify God for our good deeds. Imagine that!

They are thankful for our faith even if they don't share it. That doesn't sound like a posture of sustained hostility. For the isolationists, Peter reminds us that our good lives are lived "among the pagans." Isolation as a posture isn't righteous or even possible. For the accommodationists, Peter reminds us that we are foreigners and exiles. Foreigners and exiles tend to stick out even when they try to blend in. They can't help but be distinct. Our core posture as followers of Jesus—as a "royal priesthood" (1 Peter 2:9), as engaged exiles (Jeremiah 29:7), as reconciled reconcilers (2 Corinthians 5:18–21)—positions us for multiple gestures rather than focusing on one.

How Do We Engage?

Now that we've spent time exploring the tensions and difficulties of living in the world but not of it, we can finally return to the central question: How do we engage the world with our minds? Here are three suggestions for how to think about and act toward the world.

Adopt gestures that are informed by our kingdom citizenship. We are citizens of the kingdom of heaven (Philippians 3:20). We seek the kingdom (Matthew 6:33) and pray that the kingdom will be fully realized on earth as it is in heaven (Matthew 6:10). Therefore, the gestures we adopt toward the world should be kingdom gestures. How we engage with the world is the product of how we already think about the kingdom of God. One of the best ways to learn how to engage the world, then, is to have our minds captivated by the kingdom. Learn from Jesus, study the Scriptures, and pray for the Spirit of wisdom and discernment (Ephesians 1:17). This imaginative discernment is the purpose of many of Jesus' parables.

He wanted his disciples to know what the kingdom was like and then to live in the world accordingly.

Embrace our priestly ministry. In 1 Peter 2:9, Peter calls us a "royal priesthood." His words remind us that we are in the service of the king. Our ultimate allegiance is to him and his authority. As a priesthood, we have a ministry of reconciliation (2 Corinthians 5:18), connecting people to God. We love God and the world, and we ache for them to meet. That is our mission and purpose. To be a priest in this way requires that we be distinct from yet engaged with the world. If we lack either of these qualities, then we will be ineffective in our mission.

WE LOVE GOD AND THE WORLD, AND WE ACHE FOR THEM TO MEET.

Create and cultivate. God created us to be creators ourselves and to cultivate the world that he made. Andy Crouch goes all the way back to Genesis to identify this God-intended posture toward the world: God made us to be "artists and gardeners."[30] Christians can't be known only for what they are against; they also should be a creative presence in the world. Our posture toward the world isn't merely responsive; it is creative. Engaging the world with our minds includes imagining ways to bring healing, goodness, and beauty into it. Disciples of Jesus ought to be the foremost creators and collaborators when it comes to thinking up beautiful, redemptive art and action.

Think It Through

Social media is a major influencing factor in our world. How should a Christian think about and act toward social media? Consider the four cultural gestures discussed in this chapter. How would a person who adopts each gesture approach social media? Reflect on the potential benefits of each gesture as well as potential dangers. How do we determine the proper approach for a Christian to take?

FOR REFLECTION AND DISCUSSION

1. Looking at the chart in this chapter, where would you place yourself for most situations? Do you have a default position? Are there any attitudes toward culture which you generally disagree with? Try to think of situations where those approaches toward culture might be justified.

2. Reflect on specific moments in your life where you have most felt like a foreigner or exile in this world. What is the most Christlike way for us to respond to those moments?

3. In this chapter, we talked about "imaginative discernment." What does this concept mean for how we approach the world around us?

4. Think of times you've personally observed Christians adopting a posture of cultivation and creativity. Are there ways that you can adopt a similar posture in your day-to-day life?

Discipleship of the Mind in Christian Community

He had lost another friend, and it felt good.

Good, as in ethical. "Bad company corrupts good character," states 1 Corinthians 15:33. Yet another friend had caved into theological error, and it felt *good*—righteous, noble, pure—not to be corrupted by his friend's compromise.

It felt good in other ways too. It felt good to win arguments (for God's glory, of course). There was something pleasurable in exposing and dismantling the other guy's "theology" point by point.

His favorite theologians would no doubt take the gold, silver, and bronze in the theology Olympics, but they were long dead. Many of his former friends and contemporary, one-time heroes had stumbled into one theological error after another. With so many disqualified for this or that reason, he envisioned himself standing faithfully before God on something of a winner's platform. It felt good.

In baseball terms, he was closing in on rounding *all* the theological bases—and there were more like three hundred than three—yet most of the rest of the team was struggling to round the first few bases. Theological "home" isn't just a set of ideas; it is truths embodied in a *community* of people devoted to God. But it seemed like none of the churches he had attended cared about theology, let alone *good* theology.

Most of the church members likely didn't know what the word "theology" meant. Even the seminary-trained pastors aimed for inspiring experiences over doctrinal education. *Brainless emotionalists*, he thought as he watched the mass of churchgoers sitting around him lose themselves in the concert-style "worship" and provide the laugh track to the preacher's comedy-style "sermon." Even the church he was now attending, though it had looked promising, seemed to be yet another compromising church. Their theology was leaking in a number of areas.

Too bad for them. As for him, he was secure. His theology was well-fortified against error. Every potential leak in his ark was plugged and double-caulked.

That's why when his ark started taking on water, he didn't notice. He had fortified himself against all the *problems* presented by other people, but he had lost one of the ways God protects us best: through the *presence* of other people. In trying to build immunity to the viral acceptance and redefinition of sin, he'd left behind the relationships which could have protected him against actual sin—especially against the sin of pride.

He could list and categorize all the spiritual gifts—but he could only *appreciate* a couple of them. He'd considered the kindhearted yet simpleminded theological "lightweights" at church to be dead weight. In reality, they were God's gift to help him grow limbs from a disembodied, disempowered brain.

Shored up against theological erosion? Check. Barricaded against heresy? Check. Sensitized to all the latest isms? Check.

And yet that wasn't the only list that mattered. Hope spreader? Culture engager? Faith walker? Disciple maker? These too were checks for him, but the "check" you hear your opponent say in a chess game. Are you spreading any light in the darkness—or just adding more heat into an already-scorched atmosphere? Checkmate.

We do well to note that theological inaccuracy is only one of the Devil's weapons. You can spend your life studying for the theology "final exam," only to realize there's life outside the classroom plenty full of its own dangers.

Nathaniel Hawthorne said it well in *The Scarlet Letter*: "Trusting no man as his friend, he could not recognize his enemy when the latter actually appeared."[31] Our theological bridge burner could have learned a lot from that line. Unfortunately, such a suggestion would only make him scoff, "What serious Christian reads an irreligious writer like Hawthorne?"

* * *

In this chapter, we are exploring how we can do a better job of thinking about each other. How can we think well concerning our fellow Christians? Jesus' intention was that we as Christians would be unified in him and sanctified by the truth so that the world would come to know him (see John 17:13–23). Unity in truth can be complicated, because some Christians tend to prioritize unity over truth, while others emphasize truth over unity. Figuring out how we can best relate to each other to honor Jesus' intention calls for focused thinking, and that's the point of this chapter. First, we will look at two kinds of behaviors we need to avoid, and then we'll discuss tips for handling disagreements with other Christians. Finally, we will take a quick look at political divides within the church.

Two Dangerous People in the Church

In *The Andy Griffith Show* episode "Mountain Wedding," the hillbilly Darling family is harassed by kooky troublemaker Ernest T. Bass, who has declared that he's going to marry their daughter, Charlene. The Darlings call Sheriff Andy Taylor to help with Bass, and the sheriff finds himself dealing with crazy people on every side. Taylor has to convince the Darling patriarch not to take justice (or a shotgun) into his own hands while also trying to talk sense into Bass, who communicates mainly by throwing rocks through windows and performing spoken word poetry while banging on a tuned-up gas can.[32]

Have you ever scrolled through social media and happened upon a nasty fight between evangelicals? It'll have you feeling like Sheriff Andy Taylor. There will be trigger-happy vigilantes on your right eager to deal justice to theological troublemakers, and on your left will be window-breakers throwing rocks to disrupt sacred institutions and shatter beliefs.

Both groups stir up conflict in the community, something that God finds detestable (Proverbs 6:16–19). We're all susceptible to falling into these two roles, which we'll call "heresy hunters" and "tower topplers."

The heresy hunter is the person who hawkishly watches the words of fellow Christians to confirm whether they're a heretic: *I knew it. I knew they weren't one of us. Hey, everyone!*

Guess who's a wolf in our midst! That's a dark way to seek a dopamine rush.

The tower topplers are the Christians who feel a calling to disrupt what strikes them as theological and ethical rigidness in the church. They savor Jesus' way of challenging traditions and chafing the religious leaders. Yet when it comes to the New Testament's doctrinal and ecclesial teachings found *outside* its red letters, they're not big fans. Tower topplers are often provocateurs who push the buttons of people who care about correct Christian belief; they press until they get an ugly response that allows them to say, "See! This person who claims to follow the Bible so closely—look at how un-Christlike they are!"

Tower topplers enjoy seeing fundamentalists fall and hip evangelicals exit to "exvangelicalism" as much as heresy hunters love to discover the "commie" in the ranks.

The Makings of Heresy Hunters and Tower Topplers

What makes someone a divisive heresy hunter or disruptive tower toppler? First, some important clarifications: some heresies *need* to be outed, and some towers *need* to be toppled. People who care about right doctrine aren't who we're calling "heresy hunters." People who care about challenging rigid traditions that disconnect the church from the needs of everyday people aren't who we consider "tower topplers." On both accounts, such people are best described as "Christians."

Heresy hunters and tower topplers shape constructive tools like truth and grace into battering rams. Believers must discern when a concern for truth crosses the line into eagerness for a fight and when a desire for Jesus-style table-flipping crosses the line into a game of Taunt the Traditionalist (or, worse yet, Jesus Jenga, where you pull out so many theological planks that the whole thing eventually crumbles). Tower topplers push, and heresy hunters pounce.

> HERESY HUNTERS AND TOWER TOPPLERS SHAPE TRUTH AND GRACE INTO BATTERING RAMS.

Here's what makes heresy hunters and tower topplers two of the most dangerous, divisive kinds of people in your church: they make fellow Christians *worse.*

Self-Fulfilling Prophets

These two paths are full of self-fulfilling prophecies. People in these roles *want* to find heretics. They *want* to create defensiveness. They are so eager to proclaim, "See! I told you so!" that they make it happen.

When a heresy hunter becomes hostile and suspicious toward someone they suspect might be on the fence theologically, they may end up pushing the person off the fence onto the other side. As a case in point, take the 2021 conversion of Beth Moore from Southern Baptist to Anglican. While there were important theological questions about complementarianism and egalitarianism at play, as well as the Trump political divide, you'll never convince us that unkindness (e.g., John MacArthur's "Go home" message to her) didn't play a part in her exodus to Anglicanism. Heresy hunters can be so rigorous that they create exactly what they're looking for.

It's the same with tower topplers. When you keep poking at someone's faith, their church's belief statements, their faith's traditions, and their political persuasion, it's going to take intervention from heaven to keep them from feeling defensive. By pushing and prodding, tower topplers within the church create what they're looking for: besieged fellow Christians whose defensiveness comes out in ugly ways.

With enough blows from a battering ram, what was once just a tower is forced to bolster itself into a fortress. What had always felt a bit rigid now must fortify itself into full-blown dogmatism. Then the tower toppler triumphantly proclaims, *I always knew my church was full of red-faced sectarians who are all about preserving power and not about being like Jesus.* The self-fulfilling prophecy comes into full bloom when the tower toppler ends up blaming his fellow Christian for the fight in the first place, as if it was the other guy's first choice to fight the battles in the precise places where the battering ram kept hammering.

If you think you might be functioning as a heresy hunter or tower toppler, please stop. And if heresy hunters or tower topplers are dividing the church you love, please pray. Pray that the people who lead and influence your church will help create better followers of Jesus, not worse ones.

How to Handle Debates with Fellow Christians

You're scrolling through Facebook, not looking to start anything. But then you see a provocative post aimed squarely at your theological convictions. Maybe it's, "Pro-lifers don't really care about babies," or, "The Bible is written by misogynists," or, "The real Jesus would carry a rainbow flag and march to affirm LGBTQ practices," or, "Faith deconstruction is a good thing."

Before you realize what's happening, your fingers have started typing. Fast. You check what you've written, and it looks good. You've made solid points, everything's clear, and you've even managed to squeeze a little hope-you-are-doing-well niceness into the post. You hit enter.

It doesn't go well. The other person doubles down with their own points. Soon, it becomes a back and forth with much hostility and no headway. You hope at least someone is reading the conversation with an open mind. Hopefully it's doing some good.

Nobody wants to get into a *fruitless* debate, but it happens. So how can you start a theological conversation which generates light, not just heat?

There are three points of focus which will help you frame the conversation so that it doesn't waste anybody's time. By keeping these three things in mind throughout the conversation (and by continuing to bring the discussion back to these three things), you'll walk away having had a conversation characterized by clarity, empathy, and perhaps even agreement and persuasion.

Before we get into the three points, let's not forget the most important thing of all: prayer. Pray for guidance. Pray for discernment. Pray for pure motives. Pray for the other person. If you want the conversation to be fruitful, pray.

IF YOU WANT THE CONVERSATION TO BE FRUITFUL, PRAY.

Here are the three points of focus which will bring clarity and empathy into your conversations:

One Faith

If you're conversing with a fellow Christian, keep one thing front and center: *the faith*. By that, we're referring to what Jude called "the faith once for all entrusted to the saints" (Jude 3).

No matter what you're arguing about, you want the assumption to be that you (and hopefully the other person) are making *the faith* your true north. *That's* what you're aiming for. If either of you have drifted into prioritizing your own preferences or political positions over what God has revealed, let the conversation keep steering you back to *God's* priorities. Having *the faith* be your goal encourages you to be humble and convictional, acknowledging that you're not aiming to win somebody over to *your* side; you're both aiming to align with God's truth.

Remember, though, not all faith is created equal: some versions are so weak that they aren't worth being called "the faith" at all. Some Christians have a "plate-glass faith" so rigid and fragile that a big enough rock—including questions such as "Why do bad things happen to good people?" and "Why didn't God answer my prayers?"—will shatter the whole thing. When a plate-glass faith shatters, the pieces are often restructured into whatever shape feels right. It becomes "playdough faith," usually getting molded back together into the shape of the dominant culture. People with playdough faith tend to deny that there is a "historic Christianity" to align with. Some people exaggerate the fractured nature of Christianity, claiming there's no version of Christianity which can honestly claim to be *the faith.*

However, there *is* a historic consensus within Christianity, shared by Catholics, Orthodox, and evangelical Protestants alike and expressed in the ancient creeds. There are core teachings in the Bible visible to any open-minded reader, including God's existence, the importance of holy living, Jesus' resurrection, salvation through Jesus, and the final judgment. Recognize that, outside these essentials, good Christians will have disagreements, and try to keep these clear, core teachings of the Bible as *the faith* for which you aim.

Two Questions

The Bible gives us clear answers for many theological disagreements. Take the issue of faith deconstruction: if faith deconstruction means someone is leaving behind essential beliefs of historic Christianity, then it's a bad thing. The Bible's answer here is unmistakable.

However, let's say the question being asked about faith deconstruction is more nuanced. Perhaps there are two people who both believe that leaving behind historic Christianity is a bad thing, but they're not aligned on whether the word "deconstruction" can be used in a positive way.

One person says, "A lot of people are deconstructing their faith, and this is bad. We must not encourage people to jump on the deconstruction bandwagon, so let's not use the word 'deconstruction' as a potentially good thing. It's best to encourage people to stay away from it."

The other person responds, "Since people are already deconstructing, we can use the word 'deconstruction' in a helpful way. We can encourage them to deconstruct unhealthy aspects of their faith journey while encouraging them to reconstruct their faith in a way even *more* consistent with historic Christianity."

What's the best way for these Christians to have a fruitful conversation? There are two specific questions that, when considered during a theological debate, will result in more empathy and clarity in the conversation.

Question #1: Where is this person coming from? Have you stopped to consider what hurtful experiences this person is speaking from? What unfortunate church interactions might they be reacting against? Again, take the example of deconstruction. Perhaps the person who wants to stay completely away from the word "deconstruction" has had dangerous experiences with the concept, and they want to keep other Christians from getting too cozy with something that could be dangerous to their souls. On the other hand, the person who wants to redeem the word "deconstruction" might be reacting against a Christian upbringing that was quick to call out things as evil and sinful—even when they weren't. Asking where the other person is coming from and what hurtful experiences they're speaking from is both humbling and helpful.

Question #2: Whom is this person trying to reach? Are you debating with a Christian in an urban environment who is trying to reach progressive-leaning people for Jesus? Or are you arguing with a Christian trying to reach a rural community in a red state? Perhaps your friend is trying to reach people who identify as LGBTQ with the gospel, and that's why she reacts against posts which could be taken as disparaging toward those communities. Perhaps your friend has a heart to reach people of the Muslim faith, and that's why he takes a critical stance toward a post which paints all Muslims as jihadists.

Four words will help you tremendously in getting along with your fellow Christians: "Think like a missionary." As a foreign missionary, you would try to love people as they are. Even when you find features within a culture that are troubling, you would also see features that are admirable. You would look for bridges to the gospel and echoes of the gospel story within the culture. Think like a missionary wherever God places you, and view other Christians as missionaries in their context, respecting that the people they are trying to reach will influence how they share the gospel. This will lead to fruitful conversations fueled by empathy and clarity.

Three Levels

Not every truth in the Bible is equally important. There are three levels of faith elements, which we can call "essential," "important," and "personal":

- *Essential*—There are elements in the Bible that are essential to our eternal destiny and standing with God. At the center of the bullseye is what the Bible calls the "gospel." This involves teachings we must believe to be saved (God exists, Jesus is Lord, Jesus is the risen Savior, and salvation is by grace and not human effort) and things that are true for us if we are saved (we have the indwelling of the Holy Spirit, and we have a faith that perseveres).
- *Important*—There are secondary elements in the Bible that are important for our ongoing faithfulness to

God and for living as God intended. In 1 Corinthians, Paul wrote to Christians who were clear on essential elements but were also splitting into factions, suing each other, getting drunk during the Lord's Supper, and not holding each other accountable for serious sin. Paul wrote to them about these important areas to help them grow in their faithfulness to God. Even after we are clear on the essentials of the faith, we too must help each other grow in important areas of faithfulness.

- *Personal*—There are third-level elements which are either personal preferences which God leaves for us to decide or truths about which there is a lack of decisive evidence one way or the other.

To see these categories fleshed out, read Chad's book *Christian Convictions: Discerning the Essential, Important, and Personal Elements.*

Keeping these three elements in mind will be helpful in clarifying what's worth taking a serious stand. The more essential the topic, the more is at stake. When it comes to serious error, this no-nonsense statement from James reminds us to stay full of grace and truth in these interactions because the stakes are high:

> My brothers and sisters, if one of you should wander from the truth and someone should bring that person back, remember this: Whoever turns a sinner from the error of their way will save them from death and cover over a multitude of sins. (James 5:19–20)

A Quick Word on Politics

In closing this chapter, it's worth noting that politics sometimes splits churches and Christian friendships as surely as it splits nations. Thinking carefully and well about our fellow Christians means not allowing politics to come between us if possible. One helpful way to look at this topic is with the example of church bells.

Church bells have been used throughout church history for various reasons. Bells have been rung to announce times of prayer, begin church services, mark the hours in a day, and even to announce momentous events for the community. Church bells have been used to announce a person's death and to encourage people to pray for the person's soul. John Donne's famous poem "For Whom the Bell Tolls" speaks about how, when the bell tolls for a dead person, it mourns all of humanity, not just the person who died. Bells have been a significant mainstay of church life.

During the French Revolution of the late 1700s, the revolutionists found a new use for church bells. The leaders of the French Revolution did not look kindly upon the church or its priests or its traditions, seeing them as too intertwined with the aristocracy. They saw churches as unimportant at best.

All across France, it was decreed that church bells be melted and made into what the Revolution felt was truly valuable: coins and cannons. Something sacred and beautiful was melted down into something valuable only for its political purposes.

This sad example reminds us that we owe it to each other not to fall for such a corrupt value system. We can follow the example of Jesus, who quietly withdrew after the feeding of the 5,000, when the satisfied crowd intended to make him their king by force. Jesus refused to be made into a political pawn for any particular party. He would be King, but not through their political or military maneuvers. In the same way, the church needs to remember its identity—not as a plump voting bloc but as a God-sent agent of reconciliation. We must not let political alliances hypnotize our focus or divide our allegiance. Jesus is our King, and we are each other's brothers and sisters. These truths are nonnegotiable. Our churches must continue to ring clear the sound of community, not be melted and reshaped into coins and cannons.

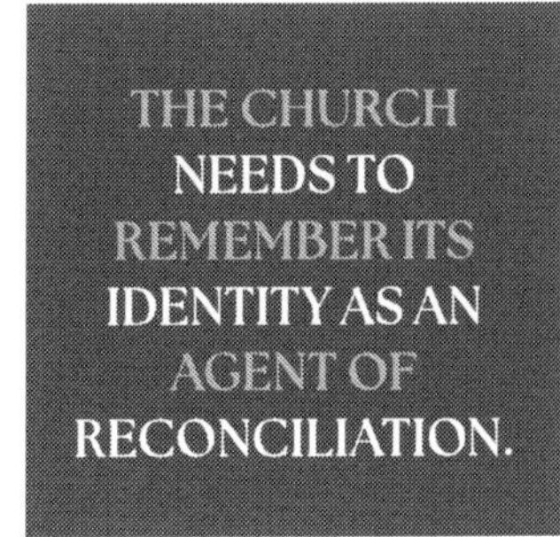

Think It Through

Here is brief exercise from Chad's book *Christian Convictions* that is useful for identifying the beliefs that are most essential. Write a short paragraph of no more than three sentences. In these three sentences, summarize the most important things you believe as a Christian. Many important beliefs won't make it into the paragraph, and that's fine. Not everything can be essential. Completing this exercise will bring clarity to our beliefs and help as we talk with other believers about issues of disagreement. Many issues that are not essential to the faith are still worth talking about, debating, and defending. However, we must think very carefully about which issues should cause deep, irreconcilable divides between brothers and sisters.

FOR REFLECTION AND DISCUSSION

1. What is "plate-glass faith" and why is it so dangerous? How do we develop a more robust and resilient faith?

2. There will obviously be disputes between Christians on all sorts of issues, both big and small. How should Christians conduct themselves in the midst of these disputes? What goals should motivate us when we find ourselves in disagreement?

3. Make a list of several practical commitments that will guide you when you find yourself disagreeing with a fellow disciple. Are any commitments different from what you would hold when disputing with a nonbeliever?

4. Worldly politics can be a wedge that divides believers and becomes an idol. Are there any other idols that we need to guard against dividing our communities?

Concluding Thoughts

In this book, we have attempted to lay the groundwork for what it looks like for disciples to love God with their whole mind. We know that even as we conclude this book we haven't said nearly enough. Our minds are wonderfully and marvelously made by God; the discipleship of our minds is not something easily summarized in a book. Our hope is that this brief work has provided some measure of guidance and inspiration as you grow in this area of your discipleship.

It's natural to end a book like this asking the question, "Where do we go from here?" What next steps can we take in learning to think well? We offer these three suggestions.

Community

We believe in the wisdom that "as iron sharpens iron, so one person sharpens another" (Proverbs 27:17). One step in learning to think Christianly is to invest yourself in a community of disciples who can mutually encourage and challenge each other in their thinking. This suggests another point, which is that our communities should be the type of communities who engage in Christian thinking. The first Christians in Acts were known for, among other things, devotion to the apostles' teaching (Acts 2:42). Our communities should not just be places where we can receive instruction on how to live the life of a Christ-follower; they should be places where we can experience a transformed mind.

Intentionality

Thinking well doesn't happen by accident. Like any positive movement in our lives, it requires a decision followed by action. We recommend you develop habits that will lead to the development of a mind fully in love with God. Read books, watch videos, or listen to podcasts that will challenge you to think more deeply about your faith and your life in this world as you follow Jesus. We live in an era with access to so many resources. Admittedly, a person must sift through a lot of less-than-helpful content to find what is truly valuable, so it is best to start with content that is recommended by trusted sources. Of course, we also have our minds shaped by becoming students of the Word. In study, meditation, and prayer, we are laid bare and transformed by God's Word (Hebrews 4:12–13). In God's Word, we are shaped by a wisdom from heaven and not from this world.

THINKING WELL DOESN'T HAPPEN BY ACCIDENT.

Practice

Related to the previous point, thinking well doesn't happen all at once. Like any discipline, it takes practice. It takes a willingness to recognize the various ways that we have tried and failed, followed by a commitment to try again. Included below is a list of characteristics of both strong and weak thinking. As you practice thinking well, this list may be helpful to gauge your progress. What isn't included in the lists below is the foundational guiding principle in the discipleship of our minds: the beginning of all wisdom is the fear of the Lord, and the end goal of all wisdom is Jesus Christ.

Ten Signs of Weak Thinking	**Ten Signs of Strong Thinking**
All or nothing thinking	*Appreciates nuance and complexity*
Open-minded to the point of cynicism	*Open-minded as an expression of curiosity*
Reflexive demonization of opponents	*Recognizes that "bad" people sometimes have good ideas and "good" people sometimes have bad ideas*
Inability to recognize any limiting principles for their ideas	*Wrestles with the long- and short-term implications of ideas*
The persistent confusion of feelings for thoughts	*Interrogates feelings rather than assuming they are always telling the truth*
Engages in personal attacks	*Charitable to others*
A posture of personal defensiveness	*A posture of humility*
Seeks victory	*Seeks understanding*
Recognizes biases in others but not in oneself	*Is able to name and address hidden assumptions both in others and in oneself*
Easily seduced by novelties and conventional wisdom	*Pursues deep and timeless truths*

Notes

1. Especially thanks to excellent tools such as Thom S. Rainer's *Autopsy of a Deceased Church: 12 Ways to Keep Yours Alive* (Nashville: B&H, 2014).

2. Mark Noll, *The Scandal of the Evangelical Mind* (Grand Rapids: Eerdmans, 1994), 3.

3. J. P. Moreland, *Love Your God with All Your Mind: The Role of Reason in the Life of the Soul* (Carol Stream, IL: NavPress, 2012), 79.

4. Moreland, 86.

5. Pope Benedict XVI, *Holy Men and Women: Of the Middle Ages and Beyond*, trans. L'Osservatore Romano (San Francisco: Ignatius, 2012), 78.

6. James Sire, *Discipleship of the Mind* (Downers Grove, IL: IVP Books, 1990), 14.

7. Alan Jacobs, *How to Think: A Survival Guide for a World at Odds* (New York: Currency, 2017), 151.

8. J. Gresham Machen, "Christianity and Culture," *Princeton Theological Review* 11, no.1 (1913): 7.

9. Moreland, 104.

10. Steve Wilkens and Mark L. Sanford, *Hidden Worldviews: Eight Cultural Stories That Shape Our Lives* (Downers Grove, IL: InterVarsity Press, 2009), 12.

11. Blaise Pascal, *Pensées*, trans. A. J. Krailsheimer (New York: Penguin Books, 1995), 37.

12. Pascal, 37.

13. "The End of Absolutes: America's New Moral Code," Barna, May 25, 2016, https://www.barna.com/research/the-end-of-absolutes-americas-new-moral-code/.

14. Carl Trueman, *Strange New World: How Thinkers and Activists Redefined Identity and Sparked the Sexual Revolution* (Wheaton, IL: Crossway, 2022), 23.

15. Trueman, 29.

16. Christian Smith and Melinda Lundquist Denton, *Soul Searching: The Religious and Spiritual Lives of American Teenagers* (Oxford: Oxford University Press, 2005).

17. Haidt specifically addresses convictions related to morality, but his observations apply beyond mere moral reasoning. Jonathan Haidt, *The Righteous Mind: Why Good People Are Divided by Politics and Religion* (New York: Vintage Books, 2012), 217.

18. Jacobs, 27.

19. Paul Copan, *Loving Wisdom: Christian Philosophy of Religion* (St. Louis, MO: Chalice, 2007), 2.

20. It is not immediately clear which person of the Trinity "him" refers to in verse seventeen since Paul mentions all three persons leading up to this pronoun. It is safe to say that "him" simply refers to God.

21. James Sire, *Habits of the Mind: Intellectual Life as a Christian Calling*, IVP Signature Collection edition (Downers Grove, IL: InterVarsity Press, 2022), 4.

22. Sire, *Habits*, 4.

23. William Lane Craig, *Reasonable Faith: Christian Truth and Apologetics* (Wheaton, IL: Crossway, 1994), 34.

24. Thomas Nagel, *The Last Word* (Oxford: Oxford University Press, 1997), 130.

25. Dallas Willard, *The Allure of Gentleness: Defending the Faith in the Manner of Jesus* (New York: HarperCollins, 2015), 21.

26. G. K. Chesterton, *Orthodoxy* (1908; repr., Colorado Springs: Waterbrook Press, 2001), 20.

27. See Guillermo Gonzalez and Jay W. Richards, *The Privileged Planet: How Our Place in the Cosmos Is Designed for Discovery* (Washington, DC: Regnery Publishing, 2004).

28. Andy Crouch, *Culture Making: Recovering Our Creative Calling* (Downers Grove, IL: InterVarsity Press, 2008).

29. Crouch, 90.

30. Crouch, 97.

31. Nathaniel Hawthorne, *The Scarlet Letter: A Romance* (London: 1851), 159.

32. James Fritzell, Everett Greenbaum, and Sheldon Leonard, *The Andy Griffith Show*, Season 3, Episode 31, "Mountain Wedding," directed by Bob Sweeney, aired April 29, 1963, Mayberry Enterprises.

About the Authors

CHAD RAGSDALE (DMin, Talbot School of Theology) is a professor and academic dean at Ozark Christian College. He is the author of *Christian Convictions* and *Holy Grit: Reflections on Hebrews for Cultivating a Faith that Lasts.* He lives with his wife and three kids in Webb City, Missouri.

DANIEL MCCOY (PhD, North-West University) is the editorial director of Renew.org. He is also a philosophy professor-at-large for Ozark Christian College. Among his books are *The Popular Handbook of World Religions* (general editor) and *Real Life Theology* (co-general editor with Bobby Harrington). He and his wife have five kids.

Made in the USA
Columbia, SC
23 April 2025